PRAYING GOD'S WILL

for
My Marriage

D0964958

LEE ROBERTS

OLIVER
NELSON

THOMAS NELSON PUBLISHERS
Nashville

To Jim and Rhonda

Published in Nashville, Tennessee, by Oliver-Nelson Books, a division of Thomas Nelson, Inc., Publishers, and distributed in Canada by Word Communications, Ltd., Richmond, British Columbia.

The Bible version used in this publication is THE NEW KING JAMES VERSION. Copyright © 1979, 1980, 1982, Thomas Nelson, Inc., Publishers. Verses have been modified to fit the prayer format.

Printed in the United States of America.

Library of Congress Cataloging-in-Publication Data

Roberts, Lee, 1941 –
    Praying God's will for my marriage / Lee Roberts.
      p. cm.
    ISBN 0-8407-9223-9 (pbk.)
     1. Married people—Prayer-books and devotions—English.
  2. Marriage—Religious aspects—Christianity.   I. Title.
BV4596.M3R634   1994   93-34311
248.8'44—dc20   CIP

1 2 3 4 5 6 — 99 98 97 96 95 94

Contents

Prayer and Your Marriage

Someone said that a successful marriage requires partners of steel. I believe that is true. But I would add that prayer is the anvil upon which the partners in a successful marriage must be shaped. If you and your spouse follow a proper plan of prayer, God will shape you according to His desires and will make your marriage everything He wants it to be.

What is a proper plan of prayer? It is simply a plan that helps you and your spouse consistently and fervently pray God's will for all areas of your relationship.

The plan before you is such a plan. In fact, it is based on the most powerful form of prayer you can use—the Word of God. God loves you so much that He revealed His will for every area of your life in His Word. For your marriage to reach the highest level possible, you and your partner must know God's will for your relationship and live accordingly. The best way to begin is to pray God's very Word, asking Him to carry out His will in your lives.

The Scripture prayers that follow contain God's perfect will for every area of your marriage. Use them to pray God's Word to Him daily. As you do, God will begin to shape you and your spouse, and He will enable you with His strength to live what you pray. Your marriage will be changed forever.

1

ANGER

Heavenly Father, in the name and power of Jesus Christ, I ask You to hear and answer my prayers concerning any anger that may exist in my spouse or me now or in the future. Help us to know and live Your words through the strength that You give us. Amen.

God, in accordance with Your word . . .

I pray that my spouse and I will be swift to hear, slow to speak, slow to wrath; for the wrath of man does not produce the righteousness of God.

JAMES 1:19–20

———— ∞ ————

I pray that our discretion will make my spouse and me slow to anger, and it is our glory to overlook a transgression.

PROVERBS 19:11

I pray that my spouse and I will commit our way to You, Lord, and trust also in You, and You shall bring it to pass. You shall bring forth our righteousness as the light, and our justice as the noonday. I pray that we will rest in You, Lord, and wait patiently for You. I pray that we do not fret because of him who prospers in his way, because of the man who brings wicked schemes to pass. I pray that we will cease from anger, and forsake wrath; that we do not fret—it only causes harm.

PSALM 37:5–8

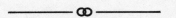

I pray that my spouse and I do not hasten in our spirits to be angry, for anger rests in the bosom of fools.

ECCLESIASTES 7:9

I pray that my spouse and I understand that a fool vents all his feelings, but a wise man holds them back.

PROVERBS 29:11

I pray that my spouse and I will let all
bitterness, wrath, anger, clamor, and evil
speaking be put away from us, with all
malice. I pray also that we will be kind
to others, tenderhearted, forgiving others,
just as God in Christ forgave us.

EPHESIANS 4:31, 32

———— ∞ ————

I pray that my spouse and I know that in
being slow to anger we are better than
the mighty, and we who rule our spirits
than he who takes a city.

PROVERBS 16:32

———— ∞ ————

I pray that my spouse and I realize that a
quick-tempered man acts foolishly.

PROVERBS 14:17

———— ∞ ————

I pray that if my spouse and I are angry, we
will not sin; that we do not let the sun
go down on our wrath.

EPHESIANS 4:26

I pray that my spouse and I will make no
friendship with an angry man, and with
a furious man will not go, lest we learn his
ways and set a snare for our souls.

PROVERBS 22:24, 25

I pray that my spouse and I always
remember that a soft answer turns away
wrath, but a harsh word stirs up anger.

PROVERBS 15:1

2
ATTITUDE

Father in heaven, give my spouse and me a proper attitude toward You, toward each other, and toward others with whom we come in contact. Give us an attitude of positive expectancy of all that we can do and be through Your power. Help us always to depend on You and Your word for our strength. Help our attitudes to be so wonderful that they bring glory to You and Your name. Amen.

God, in accordance
with Your word . . .

I pray that my spouse and I know that we can do all things through Christ who strengthens us.

PHILIPPIANS 4:13

───────── ∞ ─────────

I pray that my spouse and I will not sorrow, for the joy of the LORD is our strength.

NEHEMIAH 8:10

I pray that my spouse and I will remember whatever things are true, whatever things are noble, whatever things are just, whatever things are pure, whatever things are lovely, whatever things are of good report, if there is any virtue and if there is anything praiseworthy—that we will meditate on these things.

PHILIPPIANS 4:8

I pray that my spouse and I will remember that this is the day the Lord has made; we will rejoice and be glad in it.

PSALM 118:24

I pray that my spouse and I understand what Jesus meant when He said, "My grace is sufficient for you, for My strength is made perfect in weakness."

2 CORINTHIANS 12:9

I pray that my spouse and I realize that in all these things we are more than conquerors through Him who loved us.

ROMANS 8:37

——————— ∞ ———————

I pray that my spouse and I will always love the LORD our God with all our heart, with all our soul, with all our mind, and with all our strength and that we love our neighbor as ourselves.

MARK 12:30–31

3
CONDEMNED

Jesus, our Lord and our Savior, my spouse and I thank You for taking away our condemnations. Without You we would be condemned forever to lives of separation from the very God that created us. Thank You for the words that we now pray in this area. Amen.

**God, in accordance
with Your word . . .**

I pray that my spouse and I will draw near with a true heart in full assurance of faith, having our hearts sprinkled from an evil conscience and our bodies washed with pure water.

HEBREWS 10:22

I pray that my spouse and I always remember that You, LORD, our God, are

gracious and merciful, and that You will not
turn Your face from us if we return to
You.

2 CHRONICLES 30:9

I pray that my spouse and I know that it was
You, God, who said, "I, even I, am He
who blots out your transgressions for My
own sake."

ISAIAH 43:25

I pray in thanksgiving, God, that You did not
send Your Son into the world to
condemn my spouse and me, but that we
through Him might be saved. We who
believe in Him are not condemned.

JOHN 3:17–18

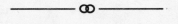

I pray that You, God, will be merciful to our
unrighteousness, and our sins and our
lawless deeds You will remember no more.

HEBREWS 8:12

I pray that my spouse and I will forsake any wicked way, and any unrighteous thoughts. Let us return to You, LORD, and You will have mercy on us and abundantly pardon us.

ISAIAH 55:7

I pray that my spouse and I acknowledge our sins to You, God, and our iniquity we do not hide, that we will confess our transgressions to You and You forgive the iniquity of our sins.

PSALM 32:5

I pray that my spouse and I who hear Your word, Jesus, and believe in Him who sent You, have everlasting life, and shall not come into judgment, but have passed from death into life.

JOHN 5:24

I pray that if my spouse and I will confess
our sins, You, God, are faithful and just
to forgive us our sins and to cleanse us from
all unrighteousness.

1 JOHN 1:9

I pray that there is therefore now no
condemnation to my spouse and me
who are in Christ Jesus, who do not walk
according to the flesh, but according to
the Spirit. For the law of the Spirit of life in
Christ Jesus has made us free from the
law of sin and death.

ROMANS 8:1–2

I pray that as far as the east is from the
west, so far have You removed our
transgressions from us.

PSALM 103:12

I pray that because my spouse and I are in
You, Christ, we are new creations; old
things have passed away; behold, all things
have become new.

2 CORINTHIANS 5:17

———— ∞ ————

I pray that my spouse and I are blessed,
whose transgressions are forgiven, whose
sins are covered.

PSALM 32:1

———— ∞ ————

I pray that my spouse and I have overcome
Satan by the blood of the Lamb and by
the word of our testimony.

REVELATION 12:11

———— ∞ ————

I pray that my spouse and I remember that
Jesus Himself said, "Neither do I
condemn you; go and sin no more."

JOHN 8:11

I pray, God, that You will forgive my spouse's and my iniquity, and our sin You will remember no more.

JEREMIAH 31:34

4
CONFIDENCE

Lord, thank You for the confidence that we have through Your power and Your strength. By ourselves we are nothing. With You we are everything. Thank You for making us more than conquerors. In Jesus' precious name we pray. Amen.

**God, in accordance
with Your word . . .**

I pray that when my spouse and I pass through the waters, You will be with us; and through the rivers, they shall not overflow us. When we walk through the fire, we shall not be burned, nor shall the flame scorch us.

ISAIAH 43:2

I pray that my spouse and I always remember that it is You, God, who justifies.

ROMANS 8:33

I pray that my spouse and I have the confidence in You, Jesus, that if we ask anything according to Your will, You hear us. And if we know that You hear us, whatever we ask, we know that we have the petitions that we have asked of You.

1 JOHN 5:14, 15

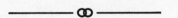

I pray that when my spouse and I face an obstacle we always remember that God has said, "Not by might nor by power, but by My Spirit."

ZECHARIAH 4:6

I pray that whatever my spouse and I ask in Jesus' name, You will do it.

JOHN 14:14

I pray that You, the LORD God, are my
spouse's and my strength.

HABAKKUK 3:19

I pray that my spouse and I will not cast
away our confidence, which has great
reward. For we have need of endurance, so
that after we have done the will of God,
we may receive the promise.

HEBREWS 10:35, 36

I pray that my spouse and I will be confident
of this very thing, that You who have
begun a good work in us will complete it
until the day of Jesus Christ.

PHILIPPIANS 1:6

I pray that my spouse and I can do all things
through Christ who strengthens us.

PHILIPPIANS 4:13

I pray that my spouse and I may boldly say:
"The LORD is our helper; we will not fear.
What can man do to us?"

HEBREWS 13:6

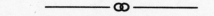

I pray that if our hearts do not condemn
us, my spouse and I have confidence
toward God.

1 JOHN 3:21

I pray that if my spouse and I will wait on
You, LORD, we shall renew our strength;
we shall mount up with wings like eagles,
we shall run and not be weary, we shall
walk and not faint.

ISAIAH 40:31

5
CONFUSED

Lord God, through the power of Your word my spouse and I call upon You to take away any confusion that may exist in either of us at any time. We know that the enemy is the author of confusion. Give us today power, love, and a sound mind. Thank You in the name of Jesus, our everything. Amen.

God, in accordance with Your word . . .

I pray that my spouse and I will trust in You, LORD, with all our heart, and lean not on our own understanding. I pray that in all our ways we will acknowledge You and You shall direct our paths.

PROVERBS 3:5, 6

I pray that You, God, will instruct my spouse
and me and teach us in the way we
should go.

PSALM 32:8

———— ∞ ————

I pray that my spouse and I have great peace
because we love Your law, and that
nothing causes us to stumble.

PSALM 119:165

———— ∞ ————

I pray that my spouse and I will always cast
our burdens on You, LORD, and You
shall sustain us.

PSALM 55:22

———— ∞ ————

I pray that when my spouse and I pass
through the waters, You will be with us.
And when we pass through the rivers, they
shall not overflow us. When we walk
through the fire, we shall not be burned, nor
shall the flame scorch us.

ISAIAH 43:2

I pray that my spouse and I will be anxious
for nothing, but in everything by prayer
and supplication, with thanksgiving, will let
our requests be made known to You,
God; and Your peace, which surpasses all
understanding, will guard our hearts and
minds through Christ Jesus.

PHILIPPIANS 4:6–7

I pray that my spouse and I will always
remember that You, God, give power to
the weak, and to those who have no might
You increase strength.

ISAIAH 40:29

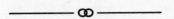

I pray that my spouse and I know that where
envy and self-seeking exist, confusion
and every evil thing are there. But the
wisdom that is from above is first pure,
then peaceable, gentle, willing to yield, full
of mercy and good fruits, without
partiality and without hypocrisy.

JAMES 3:16–17

I pray that You have not given my spouse
and me a spirit of fear, but one of power
and of love and of a sound mind.

2 TIMOTHY 1:7

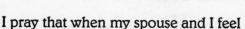

I pray that when my spouse and I feel
confused we will remember and
understand that You, God, are not the author
of confusion but of peace.

1 CORINTHIANS 14:33

I pray that You, Lord GOD, will help my
spouse and me; therefore we will not
be disgraced.

ISAIAH 50:7

I pray that my spouse and I will not think
it strange concerning the fiery trial which
is to try us, as though some strange thing
happened to us; but that we will rejoice

to the extent that we partake of Christ's
sufferings, that when His glory is
revealed, we may also be glad with
exceeding joy.

1 PETER 4:12–13

I pray that if my spouse and I lack wisdom,
we ask it of You, God, who give to all
liberally and without reproach, and that it
will be given to us.

JAMES 1:5

6

COURAGE

Heavenly Father, courage is such a powerful response to fear. Grant my spouse and me courage today and everyday. The world we live in is difficult and there is much to fear. But with You we have the courage to go into the world full of confidence and with an attitude of positive expectancy. Thank You in Jesus' name for our courage and for answering the prayers that I now pray. Amen.

God, in accordance with Your word . . .

I pray that my spouse and I will always fear not, for You, God, are with us. I pray that we will not be dismayed, for You are our God. I pray that You will strengthen us and that You will uphold us with Your righteous right hand.

ISAIAH 41:10

I pray that my spouse and I will be
persuaded that neither death nor life,
nor angels nor principalities nor powers, nor
things present nor things to come, nor
height nor depth, nor any other created
thing, shall be able to separate us from
the love of God which is in Christ Jesus our
Lord.

ROMANS 8:38–39

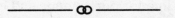

I pray that my spouse and I shall not die,
but live, and that we declare the works
of the LORD.

PSALM 118:17

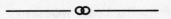

I pray that when my spouse and I pass
through the waters, You will be with us;
and through the rivers, they shall not
overflow us. When we walk through the
fire, we shall not be burned, nor shall the
flame scorch us. For You are the LORD
our God.

ISAIAH 43:2–3

I pray that You, the eternal God, are my
spouse's and my refuge, and that You
will thrust out the enemy from before us.

DEUTERONOMY 33:27

———— ∞ ————

I pray that my spouse and I can do all things
through Christ who strengthens us.

PHILIPPIANS 4:13

———— ∞ ————

I pray that my spouse and I will wait on You,
LORD; that we will be of good courage,
and that You shall strengthen our hearts.

PSALM 27:14

———— ∞ ————

I pray that if my spouse and I will wait on
You, LORD, we shall renew our strength;
we shall mount up with wings like eagles,
we shall run and not be weary, we shall
walk and not faint.

ISAIAH 40:31

I pray that my spouse and I do not think it strange concerning the fiery trial which is to try us, as though some strange thing happened to us; but that we rejoice to the extent that we partake of Christ's sufferings, that when His glory is revealed, we may also be glad with exceeding joy.

1 PETER 4:12, 13

I pray that though my spouse's and my weeping may endure for a night, joy comes in the morning.

PSALM 30:5

I pray that my spouse and I will be anxious for nothing, but that in everything by prayer and supplication, with thanksgiving, we will let our requests be made known to You.

PHILIPPIANS 4:6

I pray that my spouse and I will be of good
courage, and that You shall strengthen
our hearts, for our hope is in You, LORD.

PSALM 31:24

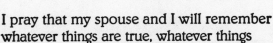

I pray that my spouse and I will remember
whatever things are true, whatever things
are noble, whatever things are just, whatever
things are pure, whatever things are
lovely, whatever things are of good report,
if there is any virtue and if there is
anything praiseworthy—that we will meditate
on these things.

PHILIPPIANS 4:8

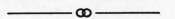

I pray that my spouse and I shall obtain joy
and gladness; and that sorrow and
sighing shall flee away.

ISAIAH 51:11

7

DELIVERANCE

Lord Jesus, use the prayers that follow to deliver
my spouse and me from any and all adversity that
we may ever face. These prayers are the very will
and words of You and our Heavenly Father. Hear
and honor them now is my prayer. In Your name I
pray. Amen.

God, in accordance
with Your word . . .

I pray that my spouse and I shall know the
truth, and the truth shall make us free.

JOHN 8:32

———— ∞ ————

I pray that because You, Jesus, make my
spouse and me free, we are free indeed.

JOHN 8:36

I pray that there is therefore now no condemnation to my spouse and me who are in Christ Jesus, who do not walk according to the flesh, but according to the Spirit. For the law of the Spirit of life in Christ Jesus has made us free from the law of sin and death.

ROMANS 8:1, 2

I pray that my spouse and I do not believe every spirit, but that we test the spirits, whether they are of You, God; because many false prophets have gone out into the world. I pray by this we will know the Spirit of God: that every spirit that confesses that Jesus Christ has come in the flesh is of God.

1 JOHN 4:1–2

I pray that He who is in my spouse and me is greater than he who is in the world.

1 JOHN 4:4

I pray that my spouse and I have overcome
Satan by the blood of the Lamb and by
the word of our testimony.

REVELATION 12:11

8

DEPRESSED

Loving God, it should not be but there are times when either or both of us suffer from some form of depression. Use Your words in the prayers that I now pray to take away any such depression from us. We pray these and all of our prayers in Jesus' name. Amen.

God, in accordance with Your word . . .

I pray that my spouse and I will cry out, and that You will hear and deliver us out of all our troubles.

PSALM 34:17

———— ∞ ————

I pray, God, that You are the God of my spouse's and my strength.

PSALM 43:2

I pray that while my spouse's and my weeping may endure for a night, our joy comes in the morning.

PSALM 30:5

I pray that if my spouse and I will wait on You, LORD, we shall renew our strength; we shall mount up with wings like eagles, we shall run and not be weary, we shall walk and not faint.

ISAIAH 40:31

I pray that neither death nor life, nor angels nor principalities nor powers, nor things present nor things to come, nor height nor depth, nor any other created thing, shall be able to separate my spouse and me from the love of God which is in Christ Jesus our Lord.

ROMANS 8:38, 39

I pray that my spouse and I do not think it
strange concerning the fiery trial which
is to try us, as though some strange thing
happened to us; but that we rejoice to
the extent that we partake of Christ's
sufferings, that when His glory is
revealed, we may also be glad with
exceeding joy.

1 PETER 4:12, 13

———————— ∞ ————————

I pray that whatever things are true,
whatever things are noble, whatever
things are just, whatever things are pure,
whatever things are lovely, whatever
things are of good report, if there is any
virtue and if there is anything
praiseworthy—that my spouse and I will
meditate on these things.

PHILIPPIANS 4:8

———————— ∞ ————————

I pray, God, that You will heal my spouse's
and my broken hearts and bind up our
wounds.

PSALM 147:3

I pray that You will comfort my spouse and
me in all our tribulation, that we may
be able to comfort those who are in any
trouble, with the comfort with which we
ourselves are comforted by You.

2 CORINTHIANS 1:4

I pray that my spouse and I will fear not,
for You are with us. That we will be
not dismayed, for You are our God. I pray
that You will strengthen us; that You will
help us and that You will uphold us with
Your righteous right hand.

ISAIAH 41:10

I pray that my spouse and I will humble
ourselves under the mighty hand of You,
God, that You may exalt us in due time. I
pray that we will cast all our care upon
You, for You care for us.

1 PETER 5:6–7

I pray that my spouse and I will always pray
and not lose heart.

LUKE 18:1

I pray that my spouse and I will not sorrow,
for the joy of the LORD is our strength.

NEHEMIAH 8:10

9

DESERTED BY LOVED ONES

Lord God, no matter what any of our loved ones may do, we know that You will never desert us. Help my spouse and me always to be aware of Your great love for us and of Your promise never to leave us and never to forsake us. Hear the prayers that follow in Jesus' name. Amen.

God, in accordance with Your word . . .

I pray that because You have set Your love upon my spouse and me, You will deliver us. You will set us on high, because we have known Your name. I pray that we shall call upon You and You will answer us. That You will be with us in trouble. That You will deliver us and honor us. That with long life You will satisfy us and show us Your salvation.

PSALM 91:14–16

I pray, God, that You will not forsake my
spouse or me, nor destroy us.

DEUTERONOMY 4:31

I pray that You, God, will hear my spouse
and me and that You will not forsake us.

ISAIAH 41:17

I pray that my spouse and I will cast all our
cares upon You, God, for You care for us.

1 PETER 5:7

I pray that while my spouse and I are hard
pressed on every side, we are not crushed;
we are perplexed, but not in despair;
persecuted, but not forsaken; struck down,
but not destroyed—always carrying about
in the body the dying of the Lord Jesus,
that the life of Jesus also may be manifested
in our bodies.

2 CORINTHIANS 4:8–10

I pray that my spouse and I shall no longer
be termed forsaken, and that You will
delight in us.

ISAIAH 62:4

———— ∞ ————

I pray that because my spouse and I know
Your name, God, we will put our trust in
You; for You, LORD, have not forsaken those
who seek You.

PSALM 9:10

———— ∞ ————

I pray that if our fathers and our mothers
forsake my spouse and me, You will take
care of us.

PSALM 27:10

———— ∞ ————

I pray that my spouse and I will be taught
to observe all things that Jesus has
commanded us and that we know that You
are with us always, even to the end of
the age.

MATTHEW 28:20

I pray that my spouse and I always
remember that You will not forget us.

ISAIAH 49:15

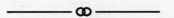

I pray that my spouse's and my hope is in
You, God, and that we shall yet praise You,
the help of our countenance and our God.

PSALM 43:5

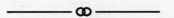

I pray that my spouse and I will be strong
and of good courage. That we will not
fear nor be afraid; for You, the LORD our God,
are the One who goes with us. We know
You will not leave us nor forsake us.

DEUTERONOMY 31:6

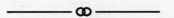

I pray that You will not forsake my spouse
and me for Your great name's sake,
because it has pleased You to make us Your
people.

1 SAMUEL 12:22

10

DISCOURAGED

Jesus, You promised the Holy Spirit as a Comforter
to us. My spouse and I need that comfort during
those periods of time when things don't always go
right and when discouragement comes upon us.
Please honor the following powerful prayers to
remove any discouragement that we might ever
face. In Your name we pray. Amen.

**God, in accordance
with Your word . . .**

I pray that my spouse and I will wait on You,
LORD; that we will be of good courage,
and that You shall strengthen our hearts.

PSALM 27:14

———— ∞ ————

I pray that my spouse and I will be of good
courage, and that You, God, shall
strengthen our hearts.

PSALM 31:24

I pray that my spouse and I shall obtain joy
and gladness and that sorrow and sighing
shall flee away.

ISAIAH 51:11

I pray that my spouse and I will not cast
away our confidence, which has great
reward. For we have need of endurance, so
that after we have done Your will, God,
we may receive the promise.

HEBREWS 10:35–36

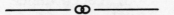

I pray that my spouse and I are confident
of this very thing, that You, God, who
have begun a good work in us will complete
it until the day of Jesus Christ.

PHILIPPIANS 1:6

I pray that my spouse and I do not grow
weary while doing good, for in due season
we shall reap if we do not lose heart.

GALATIANS 6:9

I pray that my spouse and I will greatly rejoice, though now for a little while, if need be, we may be grieved by various trials. I pray that the genuineness of our faith, being much more precious than gold that perishes, though it is tested by fire, may be found to praise, honor, and glory at Your revelation, whom having not seen we love. Though now we do not see You, Jesus, yet believing, we rejoice with joy inexpressible and full of glory, receiving the end of our faith—the salvation of our souls.

1 PETER 1:6–9

I pray that my spouse and I will be anxious for nothing, but that in everything by prayer and supplication, with thanksgiving, we will let our requests be made known to God; and the peace of God, which surpasses all understanding, will guard our hearts and minds through Christ Jesus.

PHILIPPIANS 4:6, 7

I pray that my spouse and I let not our hearts
be troubled. That we will believe in You,
God, and also in Jesus.

JOHN 14:1

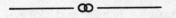

I pray that my spouse and I will always
understand and believe Your promise,
Jesus, that Your peace You left with us and
that Your peace You gave to us and that
not as the world gives did You give to us.
Let not our hearts be troubled, neither
let them be afraid.

JOHN 14:27

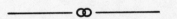

I pray that while my spouse and I are hard
pressed on every side, we are not crushed;
we are perplexed, but not in despair;
persecuted, but not forsaken; struck down,
but not destroyed—always carrying about
in the body the dying of the Lord Jesus,
that the life of Jesus also may be manifested
in our bodies.

2 CORINTHIANS 4:8–10

I pray that though my spouse and I walk in
the midst of trouble, You will revive us.
You will stretch out Your hand against the
wrath of our enemies, and Your right hand
will save us.

PSALM 138:7

11
DISSATISFIED

God, I know that my spouse and I are to be content with what we have. But sometimes we are dissatisfied. Use Your words and Your thoughts in the prayers that follow to take away our dissatisfaction. Direct our thoughts to You and to all that You have given us. In Jesus' name I pray. Amen.

God, in accordance with Your word . . .

I pray that my spouse and I can do all things through Christ who strengthens us.

PHILIPPIANS 4:13

———— ∞ ————

I pray that my spouse's and my souls shall be satisfied as with marrow and fatness, and that our mouths shall praise You with joyful lips.

PSALM 63:5

I pray that my spouse and I will be satisfied with good by the fruit of our mouths.

PROVERBS 12:14

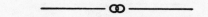

I pray that because my spouse and I seek You, LORD, we shall not lack any good thing.

PSALM 34:10

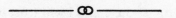

I pray that my spouse and I will bless You, LORD, with all that is within us and that we will not forget all Your benefits. I pray that we will not forget who forgives all our iniquities, who heals all our diseases. I pray that we will not forget who redeems our lives from destruction and who crowns us with lovingkindness and tender mercies and who satisfies our mouths with good things, so that our youth is renewed like the eagle's.

PSALM 103:1–5

I pray that my spouse and I will delight ourselves also in You, LORD, and You shall give us the desires of our hearts.

PSALM 37:4

———— ∞ ————

I pray that You satisfy my spouse's and my longing souls and fill our hungry souls with goodness.

PSALM 107:9

———— ∞ ————

I pray that my spouse and I will trust and not be afraid; for You, God, are our strength and song; You also have become our salvation.

ISAIAH 12:2

———— ∞ ————

I pray that You, God, who supplies seed to the sower, and bread for food, supply and multiply the seed my spouse and I have sown and increase the fruits of our righteousness.

2 CORINTHIANS 9:10

12

DISTRESS / SADNESS

Heavenly Father, sometimes things happen that bring distress and sadness into my spouse's and my lives. Use Your words to take away those times and to comfort us. Your Holy Spirit is the only comfort that can take away our distress and sadness, and we thank You for taking these times from us through the praying of Your word. In Jesus' name I pray. Amen.

God, in accordance with Your word . . .

I pray that my spouse and I have done justice and righteousness; do not leave us to our oppressors.

PSALM 119:121

————— ∞ —————

I pray that You, God, will strengthen us according to Your word.

PSALM 119:28

I pray that while my spouse and I may be small and despised, yet we do not forget Your precepts.

PSALM 119:141

I pray that while trouble and anguish have overtaken my spouse and me, Your commandments are our delights. The righteousness of Your testimonies is everlasting; give us understanding, and we shall live.

PSALM 119:143–144

I pray that in righteousness my spouse and I shall be established. That we shall be far from oppression, for we shall not fear; and from terror, for it shall not come near us.

ISAIAH 54:14

I pray that it is good for my spouse and me that we have been afflicted, that we may learn Your statutes.

PSALM 119:71

———— ∞ ————

I pray that You, God, will consider my spouse's and my affliction and deliver us, for we do not forget Your law. Plead our cause and redeem us; revive us according to Your word.

PSALM 119:153–154

———— ∞ ————

I pray that my spouse and I have great peace because we love Your law, and nothing causes us to stumble.

PSALM 119:165

———— ∞ ————

I pray that because my spouse and I have gone astray like lost sheep, You seek Your servants, for we do not forget Your commandments.

PSALM 119:176

I pray that my spouse and I will always pray "Blessed be the LORD, who daily loads us with benefits."

PSALM 68:19

———— ∞ ————

I pray that You will bring my spouse and me up out of a horrible pit, out of the miry clay, and set our feet upon a rock, and establish our steps.

PSALM 40:2

———— ∞ ————

I pray that You, God, are my spouse's and my refuge and strength, a very present help in trouble. Therefore we will not fear.

PSALM 46:1

———— ∞ ————

I pray that since Your name, LORD, is a strong tower, that my spouse and I run to it and are safe.

PROVERBS 18:10

I pray that my spouse and I will not let our hearts be troubled; that we will always believe in God and also in Jesus.

JOHN 14:1

I pray that my spouse and I will not sorrow, for the joy of the LORD is our strength.

NEHEMIAH 8:10

I pray that my spouse and I will always live with the realization that our Lord is faithful, who will establish us and guard us from the evil one.

2 THESSALONIANS 3:3

13
DON'T UNDERSTAND GOD

God, sometimes my spouse and I don't understand what You are trying to tell us. Even You tell us that Your thoughts are higher than our thoughts and Your ways are not our ways. Use the prayers that follow to reveal Yourself to us in ways that we never knew before. We ask You and we thank You in Jesus' name. Amen.

God, in accordance with Your word . . .

I pray that You, God, will help my spouse and me to understand that Your thoughts are not our thoughts, nor are our ways Your ways. That we will understand that as the heavens are higher than the earth, so are Your ways higher than our ways, and Your thoughts than our thoughts.

ISAIAH 55:8–9

I pray that my spouse and I will call to You, God, and that You will answer us, and show us great and mighty things, which we do not know.

JEREMIAH 33:3

———— ∞ ————

I pray that if You, God, are for my spouse and me, who can be against us?

ROMANS 8:31

———— ∞ ————

I pray that my spouse and I are more than conquerors through Him who loved us.

ROMANS 8:37

———— ∞ ————

I pray that as for You, God, Your way is perfect; the word of the LORD is proven; You are a shield to my spouse and me who trust in You.

PSALM 18:30

I pray that my spouse and I will pursue the knowledge of the LORD.

HOSEA 6:3

I pray, God, that You will perfect that which concerns my spouse and me and that Your mercy, O LORD, endures forever.

PSALM 138:8

I pray that You, God, will make an everlasting covenant with my spouse and me; that You will not turn away from doing us good; but You will put Your fear in our hearts so that we will not depart from You.

JEREMIAH 32:40

I pray that my spouse and I will hold fast the confession of our hope without wavering, for You who promised are faithful.

HEBREWS 10:23

I pray that all things work together for good to my spouse and me who love You, God, to us who are the called according to Your purpose.

ROMANS 8:28

I pray that no temptation has overtaken my spouse and me except such as is common to man; but You, God, are faithful, who will not allow us to be tempted beyond what we are able, but with the temptation will also make the way of escape, that we may be able to bear it.

1 CORINTHIANS 10:13

I pray that my spouse and I do not think it strange concerning the fiery trial which is to try us, as though some strange thing happened to us; but that we rejoice to the extent that we partake of Christ's sufferings, that when His glory is revealed, we may also be glad with exceeding joy.

1 PETER 4:12–13

I pray that my spouse and I will cast our burden on You, Lord, and that You shall sustain us.

PSALM 55:22

―――――― ∞ ――――――

I pray that my spouse and I will fear not, for You are with us. That we will be not dismayed, for You are our God. I pray that You will strengthen us; that You will help us, that You will uphold us with Your righteous right hand.

ISAIAH 41:10

―――――― ∞ ――――――

I pray that while many are my spouse's and my afflictions, You, Lord, deliver us out of them all.

PSALM 34:19

14

DOUBTING GOD

Lord God, may we never doubt You. My spouse and I know that You are the one consistent Being in all of creation. Help us through the praying of Your word to never doubt You. We love You and praise You in Jesus' name. Amen and Amen.

God, in accordance with Your word . . .

I pray that because Your way is perfect and Your word is proven, that You, God, are a shield to my spouse and me who trust in You.

PSALM 18:30

───────── ∞ ─────────

I pray that my spouse and I will always remember Your hand is not shortened, that it cannot save; nor Your ear heavy, that it cannot hear.

ISAIAH 59:1

I pray that You, Lord, are not slack concerning Your promise, as some count slackness, but are longsuffering toward us, not willing that any should perish but that all should come to repentance.

2 PETER 3:9

———— ∞ ————

I pray that my spouse and I are aware that You have said, "My counsel shall stand, and I will do all My pleasure. Indeed I have spoken it; I will also bring it to pass. I have purposed it; I will also do it."

ISAIAH 46:10–11

———— ∞ ————

I pray that my spouse and I know that He who calls us is faithful, who also will do it.

1 THESSALONIANS 5:24

———— ∞ ————

I pray that my spouse and I do not seek what we should eat or what we should drink, nor have anxious minds. For all these things the

nations of the world seek after, and You, our
Father, know that we need these things. I
pray that we will seek Your kingdom, God,
and all these things shall be added to us.

LUKE 12:29–31

I pray that my spouse and I will always
remember that You, God, have declared that,
"So shall My word be that goes forth from
My mouth; it shall not return to Me void,
but it shall accomplish what I please, and
it shall prosper in the thing for which I sent
it."

ISAIAH 55:11

I pray, Jesus, that my spouse and I do not
think it strange concerning the fiery trial
which is to try us, as though some strange
thing happened to us; but rejoice to the
extent that we partake of Your sufferings,
that when Your glory is revealed, we may
also be glad with exceeding joy.

1 PETER 4:12, 13

I pray that whatever things my spouse and
I ask when we pray, we will believe that
we will receive them, and we will have them.

MARK 11:24

I pray that my spouse and I know that faith
comes by hearing, and hearing by the word
of God.

ROMANS 10:17

15

EMOTIONALLY UPSET

Jesus, please use these powerful prayers from Scripture to remove every emotionally upsetting thought from my spouse and me. Give us a peace that passes all understanding and bring about an emotional calmness such as we have never before experienced. Thank You. Amen.

God, in accordance
with Your word . . .

I pray that my spouse and I will have great peace because we love Your law, and that nothing causes us to stumble.

PSALM 119:165

——————— ∞ ———————

I pray that because my spouse and I believe in You, God, we will by no means be put to shame.

1 PETER 2:6

I pray for Your help, Lord GOD, for my spouse and me; therefore we will not be disgraced. We have set our faces like a flint, and we know that we will not be ashamed.

ISAIAH 50:7

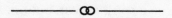

I pray that my spouse and I will be anxious for nothing, but in everything by prayer and supplication, with thanksgiving, will let our requests be made known to You, God; and Your peace, which surpasses all understanding, will guard our hearts and minds through Christ Jesus.

PHILIPPIANS 4:6–7

I pray that my spouse and I will fear not, for You are with us. That we will not be dismayed, for You are our God. I pray that You will strengthen us and help us, and uphold us with Your righteous right hand.

ISAIAH 41:10

I pray that my spouse and I will cast our burden on You, LORD, and You shall sustain us.

PSALM 55:22

I pray that You, God, have not given my spouse and me a spirit of fear, but one of power and of love and of a sound mind.

2 TIMOTHY 1:7

I pray that when my spouse and I pass through the waters, You will be with us; and through the rivers, they shall not overflow us. When we walk through the fire, we shall not be burned, nor shall the flame scorch us. For You are the LORD our God.

ISAIAH 43:2

I pray that my spouse and I will realize that You, God, are not the author of confusion but of peace.

1 CORINTHIANS 14:33

I pray that while my spouse's and my weeping may endure for a night, our joy comes in the morning.

PSALM 30:5

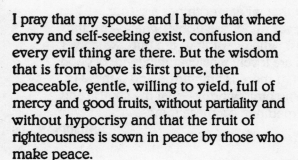

I pray that my spouse and I know that where envy and self-seeking exist, confusion and every evil thing are there. But the wisdom that is from above is first pure, then peaceable, gentle, willing to yield, full of mercy and good fruits, without partiality and without hypocrisy and that the fruit of righteousness is sown in peace by those who make peace.

JAMES 3:16–18

I pray that You, God, will comfort us in all our tribulation, that we may be able to comfort those who are in any trouble, with the comfort with which we ourselves are comforted by You.

2 CORINTHIANS 1:4

I pray that You, God, will heal my spouse's and my broken hearts and bind up our wounds.

PSALM 147:3

I pray that whatever things are true, whatever things are noble, whatever things are just, whatever things are pure, whatever things are lovely, whatever things are of good report, if there is any virtue and if there is anything praiseworthy—that my spouse and I will meditate on these things.

PHILIPPIANS 4:8

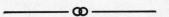

I pray that neither death nor life, nor angels nor principalities nor powers, nor things present nor things to come, nor height nor depth, nor any other created thing, shall be able to separate my spouse and me from the love of God which is in Christ Jesus our Lord.

ROMANS 8:38, 39

16
FAITH

Lord God, faith is the key to believing. Use Your words that follow to give my spouse and me more faith than we ever thought possible. Thank You, God, in Jesus' name for our faith. Amen.

God, in accordance with Your word . . .

I pray that You, Lord, will increase my spouse's and my faith.

LUKE 17:5

———— ∞ ————

I pray that my spouse's and my faith comes by hearing, and hearing by the word of God.

ROMANS 10:17

———— ∞ ————

I pray that my spouse and I will walk by faith, not by sight.

2 CORINTHIANS 5:7

I pray that my spouse and I will have a pure heart, from a good conscience, and from sincere faith.

1 TIMOTHY 1:5

———— ∞ ————

I pray that my spouse and I will always remember that faith is the substance of things hoped for, the evidence of things not seen.

HEBREWS 11:1

———— ∞ ————

I pray that my spouse and I remember that faith by itself, if it does not have works, is dead.

JAMES 2:17

———— ∞ ————

I pray that my spouse and I will constantly take the shield of faith with which we will be able to quench all the fiery darts of the wicked one.

EPHESIANS 6:16

I pray that my spouse and I will put on the breastplate of faith and love, and as a helmet the hope of salvation.

1 THESSALONIANS 5:8

———— ∞ ————

I pray that my spouse and I will always have faith and a good conscience.

1 TIMOTHY 1:19

———— ∞ ————

I pray that my spouse and I will fight the good fight of faith, that we will lay hold on eternal life, to which we were also called.

1 TIMOTHY 6:12

———— ∞ ————

I pray that my spouse and I will draw near with a true heart in full assurance of faith, having our hearts sprinkled from an evil conscience and our bodies washed with pure water.

HEBREWS 10:22

I pray that my spouse and I understand that without faith it is impossible to please You, God, for he who comes to God must believe that He is, and that He is a rewarder of those who diligently seek Him.

HEBREWS 11:6

———— ∞ ————

I pray that my spouse and I will be just and will live by faith.

HABAKKUK 2:4

———— ∞ ————

I pray that my spouse and I will remember that Abraham believed God, and it was accounted to him for righteousness.

ROMANS 4:3

———— ∞ ————

I pray that my spouse and I, having been justified by faith, will have peace with God through our Lord Jesus Christ.

ROMANS 5:1

I pray that my spouse and I will count all things loss for the excellence of the knowledge of Christ Jesus our Lord, for whom we have suffered the loss of all things, and count them as rubbish, that we may gain Christ and be found in Him, not having our own righteousness, which is from the law, but that which is through faith in Christ, the righteousness which is from God by faith; that we may know Him and the power of His resurrection, and the fellowship of His sufferings, being conformed to His death.

PHILIPPIANS 3:8–10

I pray that my spouse and I will be just and will live by faith.

HEBREWS 10:38

I pray that my spouse and I shall believe You, the LORD our God, and that we shall be established. I pray also that we will believe Your prophets, and we shall prosper.

2 CHRONICLES 20:20

I pray that according to our faith, let it be
to my spouse and me.

MATTHEW 9:29

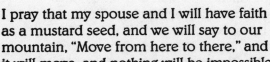

I pray that my spouse and I will have faith
as a mustard seed, and we will say to our
mountain, "Move from here to there," and
it will move; and nothing will be impossible
for us.

MATTHEW 17:20

I pray that my spouse and I will have faith
in You, God.

MARK 11:22

I pray for my spouse and me even the
righteousness of God, through faith in Jesus
Christ.

ROMANS 3:22

I pray, God, that in Your forbearance You have passed over the sins that were previously committed by my spouse and me.

ROMANS 3:25

———————— ⚭ ————————

I pray that my spouse and I will watch and that we will stand fast in the faith and that we will be brave and strong.

1 CORINTHIANS 16:13

———————— ⚭ ————————

I pray that my spouse and I will examine ourselves as to whether we are in the faith and that we will test ourselves.

2 CORINTHIANS 13:5

———————— ⚭ ————————

I pray that my spouse and I know that we are not justified by the works of the law but by faith in Jesus Christ.

GALATIANS 2:16

I pray that my spouse and I will remember that though we have the gift of prophecy and understand all mysteries and all knowledge, and though we have all faith so that we could remove mountains, if we have not love, we are nothing.

1 CORINTHIANS 13:2

I pray that my spouse and I have been crucified with Christ; it is no longer we who live, but Christ lives in us; and the life which we now live in the flesh we live by faith in the Son of God, who loved us and gave Himself for us.

GALATIANS 2:20

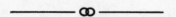

I pray that my spouse and I know the Holy Scriptures, which are able to make us wise for salvation through faith which is in Christ Jesus.

2 TIMOTHY 3:15

I pray that my spouse and I will fight the good fight, finish the race, and keep the faith.

2 TIMOTHY 4:7

———— ∞ ————

I pray that the sharing of my spouse's and my faith may become effective by the acknowledgment of every good thing which is in us in Christ Jesus.

PHILEMON 1:6

———— ∞ ————

I pray that it is by faith that my spouse and I understand that the worlds were framed by the word of God, so that the things which are seen were not made of things which are visible.

HEBREWS 11:3

———— ∞ ————

I pray that my spouse and I understand that as the body without the spirit is dead, so faith without works is dead also.

JAMES 2:26

I pray that my spouse and I will always look unto Jesus, the author and finisher of our faith, who for the joy that was set before Him endured the cross, despising the shame, and has sat down at the right hand of the throne of God.

HEBREWS 12:2

I pray that my spouse and I will realize that if we will not believe, surely we shall not be established.

ISAIAH 7:9

17

FEAR

Lord God, fear is a very real emotion. Sometimes it can be so real that it makes us unproductive in every way. But You have told us to fear not. Take now these Your very words and use them to remove any fears that my spouse and I may have. We thank You for answering our prayers in Jesus' name. Amen.

God, in accordance
with Your word . . .

I pray that Your truth shall be shield and buckler for my spouse and me, and that we shall not be afraid.

PSALM 91:4–5

I pray that no evil shall befall my spouse and me.

PSALM 91:10

I pray that my spouse and I will not be afraid of sudden terror, nor of trouble from the wicked when it comes. I pray that You, LORD, will be our confidence, and will keep our foot from being caught.

PROVERBS 3:25–26

———— ∞ ————

I pray that in righteousness my spouse and I shall be established; we shall be far from oppression, for we shall not fear; and from terror, for it shall not come near us.

ISAIAH 54:14

———— ∞ ————

I pray that in You, God, my spouse and I have put our trust; we will not be afraid.

PSALM 56:11

———— ∞ ————

I pray that my spouse and I know that You, God, have not given us a spirit of fear, but of power and of love and of a sound mind.

2 TIMOTHY 1:7

I pray that my spouse and I did not receive the spirit of bondage again to fear, but that we received the Spirit of adoption by whom we cry out, "Abba, Father."

ROMANS 8:15

———— ∞ ————

I pray that my spouse and I know that there is no fear in love; but that perfect love casts out fear.

1 JOHN 4:18

———— ∞ ————

I pray that You, God, will give Your angels charge over my spouse and me to keep us in all our ways.

PSALM 91:11

———— ∞ ————

I pray that though my spouse and I walk through the valley of the shadow of death, we will fear no evil; for You are with us; Your rod and Your staff, they comfort us.

PSALM 23:4

I pray that my spouse and I will be of good courage, and that You, God, shall strengthen our hearts, for our hope is in the LORD.

PSALM 31:24

I pray that my spouse and I receive the peace that You, Jesus, have left with us, the peace You gave to us. Let not our hearts be troubled, neither let them be afraid.

JOHN 14:27

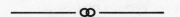

I pray that You, LORD, are my spouse's and my light and our salvation. Whom shall we fear? Though an army may encamp against us, our hearts shall not fear; in this we will be confident.

PSALM 27:1, 3

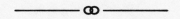

I pray that You, LORD, are my spouse's and my helper and that we will not fear.

HEBREWS 13:6

I pray that if You, God, are for my spouse and me, who can be against us? Who shall separate us from the love of Christ? Shall tribulation, or distress, or persecution, or famine, or nakedness, or peril, or sword? Yet in all these things we are more than conquerors through Him who loved us. I pray that my spouse and I will be persuaded that neither death nor life, nor angels nor principalities nor powers, nor things present nor things to come, nor height nor depth, nor any other created thing, shall be able to separate us from the love of God which is in Christ Jesus our Lord.

ROMANS 8:31, 35, 37–39

18

FINANCIAL PROBLEMS

Heavenly Father, financial problems can have such an adverse effect on us in so many ways. Unless You are trying to teach us something we ask You to remove the obstacle of financial problems and burdens from our lives. I offer up to You now Your very words to overcome any financial problems that may come our way at any time. Thank You in Jesus' name. Amen.

God, in accordance
with Your word . . .

I pray that my spouse and I may prosper
in all things and be in health, just as our
souls prosper.

3 JOHN 1:2

──────── ∞ ────────

I pray that You, LORD, are my spouse's and
my shepherd and that we shall not want.

PSALM 23:1

I pray that my spouse and I will seek You, LORD, and shall not lack any good thing.

PSALM 34:10

I pray that all these blessings shall come upon us and overtake us, because we obey the voice of the LORD our God. We shall be blessed in the city, and we shall be blessed in the country. We shall be blessed when we come in, and blessed when we go out. I pray that You, LORD, will command Your blessing on us in Your storehouses and in all to which we set our hands.

DEUTERONOMY 28:2–3, 6, 8

I pray that we will give, and it will be given to us: good measure, pressed down, shaken together, and running over will be put into our bosoms. For with the same measure that we use, it will be measured back to us.

LUKE 6:38

I pray that because freely my spouse and I
have received, freely we will give.

MATTHEW 10:8

I pray that on the first day of the week my
spouse and I will lay something aside, storing
up as we may prosper, that there be no
collections when it is time to give.

1 CORINTHIANS 16:2

I pray that my spouse and I will bring all
the tithes into the storehouse, that there may
be food in Your house. And that we will try
You, God, in this and see if You will not open
for us the windows of heaven and pour out
for us such blessing that there will not be
room enough to receive it.

MALACHI 3:10

I pray that my spouse and I realize that if
we sow sparingly we will also reap sparingly,
and if we sow bountifully we will also reap

bountifully. I pray that we will give as we purpose in our hearts, not grudgingly or of necessity; for You, God, love a cheerful giver. And You are able to make all grace abound toward us, that we, always having all sufficiency in all things, may have an abundance for every good work.

2 CORINTHIANS 9:6–8

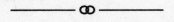

I pray that everyone who left houses or brothers or sisters or father or mother or wife or children or lands, for Your name's sake, Lord, shall receive a hundredfold, and inherit eternal life. I pray also that my spouse and I will remember that many who are first will be last, and the last first.

MATTHEW 19:29–30

I pray that my spouse and I leave an inheritance to our children's children.

PROVERBS 13:22

I pray that this Book of the Law shall not depart from my spouse's and my mouths, but that we shall meditate in it day and night, that we may observe to do according to all that is written in it. For then we will make our way prosperous, and then we will have good success.

JOSHUA 1:8

I pray that You will give wisdom and knowledge and joy to my spouse and me who are good in Your sight; but to the sinner You will give the work of gathering and collecting, that he may give to us who are good before You.

ECCLESIASTES 2:26

I pray that You shall supply all my spouse's and my needs according to Your riches in glory by Christ Jesus.

PHILIPPIANS 4:19

I pray that my spouse and I do not worry about our lives, saying what will we eat or what will we drink; nor about our bodies, what will we put on. For You, our Heavenly Father, know that we need all these things. But we pray that we will seek first Your kingdom, God, and Your righteousness, and all these things shall be added to us. I also pray that we not worry about tomorrow, for tomorrow will worry about its own things.

MATTHEW 6:25, 32–34

19

FORGIVENESS

Jesus, my spouse and I need Your forgiveness. We never want to sin, but sometimes we do. Hear now the following prayers directly from Your word and forgive us for any and everything in our lives that is not pleasing to You. Amen.

God, in accordance with Your word . . .

I pray that as far as the east is from the west, so far have You removed my spouse's and my transgressions from us.

PSALM 103:12

──────── ∞ ────────

I pray that You blot out my spouse's and my transgressions for Your own sake; and that You will not remember our sins.

ISAIAH 43:25

I pray that my spouse and I will return to You, LORD, and You will have mercy on us; and to our God, for You will abundantly pardon.

ISAIAH 55:7

I pray that You, God, will cleanse my spouse and me from all our iniquity by which we have sinned against You, and that You will pardon all our iniquities by which we have sinned and by which we have transgressed against You.

JEREMIAH 33:8

I pray that whenever my spouse and I stand praying, if we have anything against anyone, that we will forgive him, so that You, our Father in heaven, may also forgive us our trespasses.

MARK 11:25

I pray that my spouse's and my transgression is forgiven, and our sin covered.

PSALM 32:1

I pray that in You, Jesus, my spouse and I have redemption through Your blood, the forgiveness of sins, according to the riches of Your grace.

EPHESIANS 1:7

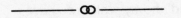

I pray that my spouse and I will bear with others, and forgive others, if we have a complaint against another; even as Christ forgave us, so we also must do.

COLOSSIANS 3:13

I pray that my spouse and I walk by faith, not by sight.

2 CORINTHIANS 5:7

I pray that if my spouse and I confess our
sins, that You, God, are faithful and just
to forgive us our sins and to cleanse us from
all unrighteousness.

1 JOHN 1:9

———————— ∞ ————————

I pray that if my spouse and I sin, we have
an Advocate with You, the Father, Jesus
Christ the righteous.

1 JOHN 2:1

20

GODLY LIFE

Lord God, more than anything else my spouse and I want to live godly lives. The only way we can ever do that is through the praying of Your powerful words and through the honoring of Your word in our lives. Hear and answer these my prayers in Jesus' name. Amen.

God, in accordance with Your word . . .

I pray that if my spouse and I live, we live to You, the Lord; and if we die, we die to You. Therefore, whether we live or die, we are Yours, Lord.

ROMANS 14:8

———————— ∞ ————————

I pray that my spouse and I believe on You, Jesus, who justifies the ungodly, that our faith is accounted for righteousness.

ROMANS 4:5

I pray that what the law could not do in
my spouse and me in that it was weak
through the flesh, You, God, did by sending
Your own Son in the likeness of sinful
flesh, on account of sin: You condemned
sin in the flesh, that the righteous
requirement of the law might be fulfilled
in us who do not walk according to the
flesh but according to the Spirit.

ROMANS 8:3–4

I pray that my spouse and I will present our
bodies a living sacrifice, holy, acceptable
to You, God.

ROMANS 12:1

I pray that my spouse and I will not be
conformed to this world, but that we will
be transformed by the renewing of our
minds, that we may prove what is that
good and acceptable and perfect will of God.

ROMANS 12:2

I pray that my spouse and I do not present our members as instruments of unrighteousness to sin, but present ourselves to God as being alive from the dead, and our members as instruments of righteousness to God. For sin shall not have dominion over us, for we are not under law but under grace.

ROMANS 6:13–14

I pray that my spouse and I will not think of ourselves more highly than we ought to think, but to think soberly, as You, God, have dealt to us a measure of faith.

ROMANS 12:3

I pray that because You, Christ, are in my spouse and me, our bodies are dead because of sin, but the Spirit is life because of righteousness.

ROMANS 8:10

I pray that my spouse and I know that because You predestined us, You also called us; that because You called us, You also justified us; that because You justified us, You also glorified us.

ROMANS 8:30

———————— ∞ ————————

I pray that because my spouse and I are in You, Christ, we are new creations; old things have passed away; behold, all things have become new.

2 CORINTHIANS 5:17

———————— ∞ ————————

I pray that You, God, made Jesus, who knew no sin, to be sin for us, that we might become the righteousness of You in Him.

2 CORINTHIANS 5:21

———————— ∞ ————————

I pray that my spouse and I will remain in the same calling in which we were called.

1 CORINTHIANS 7:20

I pray that You are able to make all grace
abound toward my spouse and me, that
we, always having all sufficiency in all things,
may have an abundance for every good
work.

2 CORINTHIANS 9:8

———————— ⨉ ————————

I pray that if my spouse and I glory, we will
glory in You, Lord.

1 CORINTHIANS 1:31

———————— ⨉ ————————

I pray that my spouse and I will not let sin
reign in our mortal bodies, that we should
obey it in its lusts.

ROMANS 6:12

———————— ⨉ ————————

I pray that my spouse and I know that since
we have been set free from sin, we have
become slaves of God.

ROMANS 6:22

I pray that my spouse and I will be renewed
in the spirit of our minds, and that we
will put on the new man which was created
according to You, God, in true
righteousness and holiness.

EPHESIANS 4:23–24

———— ∞ ————

I pray that it is good for my spouse and me
to draw near to God; to put our trust in
the Lord God, that we may declare all Your
works.

PSALM 73:28

———— ∞ ————

I pray that my spouse and I will delight
ourselves also in You, Lord, and that You
shall give us the desires of our hearts.

PSALM 37:4

———— ∞ ————

I pray that You, God, will satisfy my spouse's
and my mouths with good things, so that
our youth is renewed like the eagle's.

PSALM 103:5

I pray that my spouse and I are companions of all who fear You, and of those who keep Your precepts.

PSALM 119:63

———— ⊙ ————

I pray that my spouse and I are blessed because we are the undefiled in the way and walk in the law of the LORD.

PSALM 119:1

———— ⊙ ————

I pray that my spouse's and my ways are directed to keep Your statutes, God.

PSALM 119:5

———— ⊙ ————

I pray that my spouse and I will cleanse our way by taking heed according to Your word, God.

PSALM 119:9

I pray that with our whole hearts my spouse
and I have sought You, God; Oh, let us
not wander from Your commandments!

PSALM 119:10

∞

I pray that my spouse and I have hidden
Your word in our hearts, that we might
not sin against You!

PSALM 119:11

∞

I pray that my spouse and I will delight
ourselves in Your statutes, God; and that
we will not forget Your word.

PSALM 119:16

∞

I pray that You, God, will open my spouse's
and my eyes, that we may see wondrous
things from Your law.

PSALM 119:18

I pray, God, that Your testimonies also are my spouse's and my delight and our counselors.

PSALM 119:24

I pray that my spouse and I have declared our ways, and that You, God, have answered us; teach us Your statutes.

PSALM 119:26

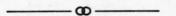

I pray that You, God, will make my spouse and me understand the way of Your precepts; so shall we meditate on Your wondrous works.

PSALM 119:27

I pray that my spouse and I have chosen the way of truth; and that Your judgments we have laid before us. I pray that we will cling to Your testimonies; O LORD, do not put us to shame!

PSALM 119:30, 31

I pray that You will make my spouse and me walk in the path of Your commandments, for we delight in it.

PSALM 119:35

⚭

I pray that my spouse and I will incline our hearts to Your testimonies, God, and not to covetousness. Turn away our eyes from looking at worthless things, and revive us in Your way.

PSALM 119:36–37

⚭

I pray that You, God, will remember the word to Your servants, my spouse and me, upon which You have caused us to hope.

PSALM 119:49

⚭

I pray that You, God, will be merciful to my spouse and me according to Your word.

PSALM 119:58

I pray, O God, that my spouse and I have thought about our ways, and turned our feet to Your testimonies. I pray that we have made haste, and did not delay to keep Your commandments.

PSALM 119:59–60

―――― ∞ ――――

I pray that You, God, will teach my spouse and me good judgment and knowledge, for we believe Your commandments.

PSALM 119:66

―――― ∞ ――――

I pray, God, that Your hands have made my spouse and me and fashioned us; give us understanding, that we may learn Your commandments.

PSALM 119:73

―――― ∞ ――――

I pray, God, that You will let Your merciful kindness be for my spouse's and my comfort.

PSALM 119:76

I pray, God, that You let my spouse's and
my hearts be blameless regarding Your
statutes, that we may not be ashamed.

PSALM 119:80

⬤⬤

I pray that my spouse and I will never forget
Your precepts, for by them You have given
us life.

PSALM 119:93

⬤⬤

I pray that Your word, O God, is a lamp to
my spouse's and my feet and a light to
our path.

PSALM 119:105

⬤⬤

I pray that You, God, are my spouse's and
my hiding place and our shield; we hope
in Your word.

PSALM 119:114

I pray that You, God, will give my spouse
and me understanding, that we may know
Your testimonies.

PSALM 119:125

⚭

I pray that my spouse's and my steps are
directed by Your word, God, and that You
let no iniquity have dominion over us.

PSALM 119:133

⚭

I pray that my spouse and I shall love the
Lord our God with all our heart, with all
our soul, with all our mind, and with all our
strength and that we shall love our
neighbor as ourselves.

MARK 12:30–31

⚭

I pray that You, Jesus, are at my spouse's
and my right hand, that we may not be
shaken.

ACTS 2:25

I pray that my spouse and I may gain You,
Christ, and be found in You, not having
our own righteousness, which is from the
law, but that which is through faith in You,
the righteousness which is from God by faith;
that we may know You and the power of
Your resurrection, and the fellowship of Your
sufferings, being conformed to Your death.

PHILIPPIANS 3:8–10

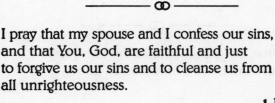

I pray that my spouse and I confess our sins,
and that You, God, are faithful and just
to forgive us our sins and to cleanse us from
all unrighteousness.

1 JOHN 1:9

I pray that my spouse's and my work of
righteousness will be peace, and the effect
of righteousness, quietness and assurance
forever.

ISAIAH 32:17

I pray that my spouse and I are blessed who
walk not in the counsel of the ungodly,
nor stand in the path of sinners, nor sit in
the seat of the scornful. But our delight
is in the law of the LORD, and in Your law
we meditate day and night. I pray that
we shall be like a tree planted by the rivers
of water, that brings forth its fruit in its
season, whose leaf also shall not wither; and
whatever we do shall prosper.

PSALM 1:1–3

I pray that my spouse and I shall know the
truth, and the truth shall make us free.

JOHN 8:32

I pray that my spouse and I take up Your
whole armor, God, that we may be able
to withstand in the evil day, and having done
all, to stand. I pray that we stand therefore,
having girded our waist with truth, having
put on the breastplate of righteousness,
and having shod our feet with the

preparation of the gospel of peace; and above all, taking the shield of faith with which we will be able to quench all the fiery darts of the wicked one. I pray that we will take the helmet of salvation, and the sword of the Spirit, which is the word of God; praying always with all prayer and supplication in the Spirit, being watchful to this end with all perseverance and supplication for all the saints.

EPHESIANS 6:13–18

───────── ∞ ─────────

I pray that my spouse and I will be diligent to present ourselves approved to You, God, as workers who do not need to be ashamed, rightly dividing the word of truth.

2 TIMOTHY 2:15

───────── ∞ ─────────

I pray that no one deceives my spouse and me with empty words.

EPHESIANS 5:6

I pray that my spouse and I will be doers of the word, and not hearers only, deceiving ourselves.

JAMES 1:22

I pray that my spouse and I will not be deceived, for You, God, are not mocked; for whatever we sow, that we will also reap.

GALATIANS 6:7

I pray that my spouse and I will always remember that all Scripture is given by inspiration of You, God, and is profitable for doctrine, for reproof, for correction, for instruction in righteousness, that the man of God may be complete, thoroughly equipped for every good work.

2 TIMOTHY 3:16–17

21

GOD'S LOVE

God, grant my spouse and me the wonders of Your love. We want Your love so much. I come now to pray the following prayers directly from Your word to petition You for Your love. And I do it in Jesus' name. Amen.

God, in accordance with Your word . . .

I pray that my spouse and I know that love is not that we loved You, God, but that You loved us and sent Your Son to be the propitiation for our sins.

1 JOHN 4:10

———————— ∞ ————————

I pray that my spouse and I love You because You first loved us.

1 JOHN 4:19

I pray that You, Christ, may dwell in our hearts through faith; that we, being rooted and grounded in love, may be able to comprehend with all the saints what is the width and length and depth and height—to know Your love, Christ, which passes knowledge; that we may be filled with all the fullness of God.

EPHESIANS 3:17–19

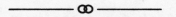

I pray that my spouse and I never forget that You, God, demonstrated Your own love toward us, in that while we were still sinners, Christ died for us.

ROMANS 5:8

I pray that You, God, so loved my spouse and me that You gave Your only begotten Son, that we who believe in Him should not perish but have everlasting life.

JOHN 3:16

I pray that neither death nor life, nor angels nor principalities nor powers, nor things present nor things to come, nor height nor depth, nor any other created thing, shall be able to separate my spouse and me from Your love, God, which is in Christ Jesus our Lord.

ROMANS 8:38–39

———— ∞ ————

I pray that my spouse and I have Your commandments, Jesus, and keep them, as those who love You. And because we love You, we will be loved by Your Father, and You will love us and manifest Yourself to us.

JOHN 14:21

———— ∞ ————

I pray that my spouse and I know that You, God, have loved us with an everlasting love; therefore with lovingkindness You have drawn us.

JEREMIAH 31:3

I pray that my spouse and I realize that You,
God, will rejoice over us with gladness,
You will quiet us with Your love, You will
rejoice over us with singing.

ZEPHANIAH 3:17

22

GOD'S WORD

Heavenly Father, thank You for Your word. It is so important to my spouse and me to be able to pray Your word as a part of our daily life. Please honor now the praying of Your word in Jesus' name. Amen.

God, in accordance with Your word . . .

I pray that in my spouse's and my life Your word is living and powerful, and sharper than any two-edged sword, piercing even to the division of soul and spirit, and of joints and marrow, and is a discerner of the thoughts and intents of our hearts.

HEBREWS 4:12

———————— ∞ ————————

I pray that my spouse and I will never forget that the word of the Lord endures forever.

1 PETER 1:25

I pray that my spouse and I having been
born again, are not of corruptible seed
but incorruptible, through the word of God
which lives and abides forever.

1 PETER 1:23

I pray that my spouse and I put into practice
the fact that we shall not live by bread
alone, but by every word that proceeds from
the mouth of God.

MATTHEW 4:4

I pray that my spouse and I will always
understand and apply the fact that all
Scripture is given by Your inspiration, God,
and is profitable for doctrine, for reproof,
for correction, for instruction in
righteousness.

2 TIMOTHY 3:16

I pray that my spouse and I know that we have been given exceedingly great and precious promises, that through these we may be partakers of the divine nature, having escaped the corruption that is in the world through lust.

2 PETER 1:4

I pray that my spouse and I always remember that heaven and earth will pass away, but Your words, Jesus, will by no means pass away.

MATTHEW 24:35

I pray that my spouse and I understand the significance of the fact that till heaven and earth pass away, one jot or one tittle will by no means pass from the law till all is fulfilled.

MATTHEW 5:18

I pray that my spouse and I take to heart
the fact that heaven and earth will pass
away, but Your words, Jesus, will by no
means pass away.

MARK 13:31

———— ∞ ————

I pray that my spouse and I will abide in
Your words, Jesus, and be Your disciples.
And we shall know the truth, and the truth
shall make us free.

JOHN 8:31, 32

———— ∞ ————

I pray that my spouse's and my walk with
You, LORD, may be so close that our ears
shall hear a word behind saying, "This is the
way, walk in it."

ISAIAH 30:21

———— ∞ ————

I pray that You, O God, will instruct my
spouse and me and teach us in the way
we should go and guide us with Your eye.

PSALM 32:8

I pray that my spouse and I will give attention to Your words, O God, that we will incline our ears to Your sayings. Do not let them depart from our eyes; keep them in the midst of our hearts; for they are life to those who find them, and health to all their flesh.

PROVERBS 4:20–22

I pray, God, that my spouse and I will know that Your every word is pure and that You are a shield to those who put their trust in You. I pray that we will not add to Your words, lest You reprove us, and we be found liars.

PROVERBS 30:5–6

I pray that my spouse and I realize the significance of the fact that You, God, said, "So shall My word be that goes forth from My mouth; it shall not return to Me void."

ISAIAH 55:11

I pray that my spouse and I will not be like the horse or like the mule, which have no understanding, which must be harnessed with bit and bridle, else they will not come near you.

PSALM 32:9

I pray, God, that my spouse and I will not let Your Book of the Law depart from our mouths, but we shall meditate in it day and night, that we may observe to do according to all that is written in it. For then we will make our way prosperous, and then we will have good success.

JOSHUA 1:8

I pray, O God, that my spouse and I will take Your testimonies as a heritage forever, for they are the rejoicing of our hearts.

PSALM 119:111

I pray that my spouse and I are Your
servants, O God; give us understanding,
that we may know Your testimonies.

PSALM 119:124

23

GRIEF / HURTING

Jesus, sometimes my spouse and I hurt. Sometimes we go through periods of grief. Use now Your own words that I pray to remove any grief or any hurts that we may have now or in the future. I pray to You in Your name. Amen.

God, in accordance
with Your word . . .

I pray that You, God, will comfort my spouse and me who mourn and to give us beauty for ashes, the oil of joy for mourning, the garment of praise for the spirit of heaviness; that we may be called trees of righteousness.

ISAIAH 61:2, 3

———— ∞ ————

I pray that my spouse and I are blessed when we mourn, for we shall be comforted.

MATTHEW 5:4

I pray, O God, that You will comfort my
spouse and me in all our tribulation, that
we may be able to comfort those who are
in any trouble, with the comfort with
which we ourselves are comforted by You.

2 CORINTHIANS 1:4

——————— ∞ ———————

I pray that my spouse and I will not be
ignorant concerning those who have
fallen asleep, lest we sorrow as others who
have no hope.

1 THESSALONIANS 4:13

——————— ∞ ———————

I pray, O God, that You have comforted my
spouse and me and will have mercy on
our afflictions.

ISAIAH 49:13

——————— ∞ ———————

I pray that when my spouse and I pass
through the waters, You will be with us;
and through the rivers, they shall not

overflow us. When we walk through the
fire, we shall not be burned, nor shall the
flame scorch us.

ISAIAH 43:2

I pray that the Lord Jesus Christ Himself, and,
You, our God and Father, who have loved
us and given us everlasting consolation and
good hope by grace, comfort our hearts
and establish us in every good word and
work.

2 THESSALONIANS 2:16–17

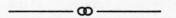

I pray that my spouse and I always
remember that in You, Jesus, we do not
have a High Priest who cannot sympathize
with our weaknesses, but was in all points
tempted as we are, yet without sin. Let us
therefore come boldly to the throne of
grace, that we may obtain mercy and find
grace to help in time of need.

HEBREWS 4:15, 16

I pray that though my spouse and I walk through the valley of the shadow of death, we will fear no evil; for You are with us; Your rod and Your staff, they comfort us.

PSALM 23:4

———— ∞ ————

I pray that in this crucial time in my spouse's and my life we can say, "O Death, where is your sting? O Hades, where is your victory?"

1 CORINTHIANS 15:55

———— ∞ ————

I pray that this is my spouse's and my comfort in our affliction, for Your word has given us life.

PSALM 119:50

———— ∞ ————

I pray that my spouse and I will cast all our care upon You, O God, for You care for us.

1 PETER 5:7

I pray that You, God, will wipe away every tear from my spouse's and my eyes and that there shall be no more death, nor sorrow, nor crying. I pray that there shall be no more pain, for the former things have passed away.

REVELATION 21:4

I pray that we will fear not, for You are with us; nor be dismayed, for You are our God. I pray that You will strengthen us and help us and will uphold us with Your righteous right hand.

ISAIAH 41:10

I pray that my spouse and I will walk by faith and not by sight and that we are confident, yes, well pleased rather to be absent from the body and to be present with the Lord.

2 CORINTHIANS 5:7, 8

I pray that my spouse and I shall obtain joy
and gladness; sorrow and sighing shall flee
away.

ISAIAH 51:11

24

INHERITANCE

Heavenly Father, in Jesus' name I thank You for the inheritance that You have provided for my spouse and me. Never let us forget it. Hear now Your words on the subject of our inheritance. Amen.

God, in accordance with Your word . . .

I pray that whatever my spouse and I do, we do it heartily, as to the Lord and not to men, knowing that from the Lord we will receive the reward of the inheritance; for we serve the Lord Christ.

COLOSSIANS 3:23–24

—— ∞ ——

I pray that my spouse and I have an inheritance incorruptible and undefiled and that does not fade away, reserved in heaven for us.

1 PETER 1:4

I pray that my spouse and I have been given
exceedingly great and precious promises,
that through these we may be partakers of
the divine nature, having escaped the
corruption that is in the world through lust.

2 PETER 1:4

I commend my spouse to you, God, and
to the word of Your grace, which is able
to build us up and give us an inheritance
among all those who are sanctified.

ACTS 20:32

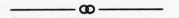

I pray, God, that the Spirit Himself bears
witness with my spouse's and my spirits
that we are children of God, and if children,
then heirs—heirs of God and joint heirs
with Christ, if indeed we suffer with Him,
that we may also be glorified together.

ROMANS 8:16–17

I pray that my spouse and I are in You, Jesus, and have obtained an inheritance, being predestined according to Your purpose, who works all things according to the counsel of Your will, that we who first trusted in You should be to the praise of Your glory. In You, Jesus, we also trusted, after we heard the word of truth, the gospel of our salvation; in whom also, having believed, we were sealed with the Holy Spirit of promise, who is the guarantee of our inheritance until the redemption of the purchased possession, to the praise of Your glory.

EPHESIANS 1:11–14

I pray, Lord, that my spouse and I are aware that eye has not seen, nor ear heard, nor have entered into the heart of man the things which You have prepared for those who love You.

1 CORINTHIANS 2:9

I pray that my spouse and I always remember, Jesus, that in Your Father's house, are many mansions; if it were not so, You would have told us. Help us to remember that You have gone to prepare a place for us. And if You go and prepare a place for us, You will come again and receive us to Yourself; that where You are, there we may be also.

JOHN 14:2-3

25

LONELY

Lord, I pray Your very words from Scripture to ask You to take away any lonely feelings that my spouse and I may ever have. Your word is clear that You will never leave us or forsake us and that You will always be our constant companion. Thank You, Lord, for the assurance of Your words. Amen.

God, in accordance
with Your word . . .

I pray that my spouse's and my conduct be without covetousness; that we be content with such things as we have. For You, God, have said, "I will never leave you nor forsake you."

HEBREWS 13:5

———— ∞ ————

I pray that my spouse and I remember Jesus' promise to be with us always, even to the end of the age.

MATTHEW 28:20

I pray that my spouse and I will fear not,
for You are with us; nor be dismayed, for
You are our God. I pray that You will
strengthen us with Your righteous right
hand.

ISAIAH 41:10

I pray that my spouse and I realize that You,
God, count the number of the stars and
call them all by name. I pray that we
remember that You are great and mighty
in power and Your understanding is infinite.

PSALM 147:4–5

I pray that neither death nor life, nor angels
nor principalities nor powers, nor things
present nor things to come, nor height nor
depth, nor any other created thing, shall
be able to separate my spouse and me from
the love of God which is in You, Christ
Jesus.

ROMANS 8:38–39

I pray, Jesus, that my spouse and I remember Your promise that You will not leave us orphans; You will come to us.

JOHN 14:18

I pray that my spouse and I will be strong and of good courage, and that we do not fear nor are we afraid, for You, the LORD our God, You are the One who goes with us. I pray that You will not leave us nor forsake us.

DEUTERONOMY 31:6

I pray that if our fathers and mothers forsake us, then You, LORD, will take care of my spouse and me.

PSALM 27:10

I pray, O God, that my spouse and I remember You are our refuge and strength, a very present help in trouble.

PSALM 46:1

I pray that though the mountains shall depart and the hills be removed, Your kindness, God, shall not depart from my spouse and me, nor shall Your covenant of peace be removed.

ISAIAH 54:10

26

LOVE

Jesus, You are love. I pray now Your words and the words of Your Father that my spouse and I will know and experience Your love and that we will love others as we love ourselves and each other. Teach us to love as You would have us to love. In Your name I pray. Amen.

God, in accordance
with Your word . . .

I pray that my spouse and I will love others, for love is of You, God.

1 JOHN 4:7

———— ∞ ————

I pray that my spouse and I know that You, God, sent Your Son to be the propitiation for our sins. And help us to know that if You so loved us, we also ought to love one another.

1 JOHN 4:10–11

I pray that my spouse and I totally understand that as You, God, loved Jesus, You also love us and we are to abide in Your love.

JOHN 15:9

———— ∞ ————

I pray that my spouse and I have Your commandments, Jesus, and keep them, and that we love You. And we who love You will be loved by Your Father, and You will love us and manifest Yourself to us.

JOHN 14:21

———— ∞ ————

I pray, God, that You have loved my spouse and me with an everlasting love; and with lovingkindness You have drawn us.

JEREMIAH 31:3

———— ∞ ————

I pray that You, God, love my spouse and me because we have loved Jesus, and have believed that Jesus came forth from You.

JOHN 16:27

I pray that my spouse and I shall love You,
the Lord our God, with all our heart, with
all our soul, with all our mind, and with all
our strength and that we shall love our
neighbor as ourselves.

MARK 12:30–31

I pray that my spouse and I have known
and believed the love that You, God, have
for us; and that we who love God must love
our brother also.

1 JOHN 4:16, 21

I pray that my spouse and I understand the
true meaning of love and that though we
speak with the tongues of men and of angels,
but have not love, we have become
sounding brass or a clanging cymbal. And
though we have the gift of prophecy, and
understand all mysteries and all knowledge,
and though we have all faith, so that we
could remove mountains, but have not love,
we are nothing. And though we bestow all

our goods to feed the poor, and though we
give our bodies to be burned, but have not
love, it profits us nothing. I pray that we
remember that love suffers long and is kind;
love does not envy; love does not parade
itself, is not puffed up; does not behave
rudely, does not seek its own, is not
provoked, thinks no evil; does not rejoice
in iniquity, but rejoices in the truth; bears
all things, believes all things, hopes all things,
endures all things. Help us to understand
that love never fails. Help us to know that
there abide faith, hope, love, these three;
but the greatest of these is love.

1 CORINTHIANS 13:1–8, 13

I pray that neither death nor life, nor angels
nor principalities nor powers, nor things
present nor things to come, nor height nor
depth, nor any other created thing, shall be
able to separate my spouse and me from
the love of God which is in Christ Jesus our
Lord.

ROMANS 8:38–39

I pray, Jesus, that my spouse and I will take
heed to the new commandment You gave
to us, that we love one another; as You have
loved us, that we also love one another. By
this all will know that we are Your disciples,
if we have love for one another.

JOHN 13:34–35

I pray that my spouse and I will realize that
You, God, demonstrated Your own love
toward us, in that while we were still sinners,
Christ died for us.

ROMANS 5:8

I pray that You, God, so loved my spouse
and me that You gave Your only begotten
Son, Jesus, that we who believe in Jesus
should not perish but have everlasting life.

JOHN 3:16

I pray that my spouse and I know that it is Your commandment, Jesus, that we love one another as You have loved us.

JOHN 15:12

———— ∞ ————

27

LOVE FOR MY SPOUSE

Lord, I pray these Your words for my spouse and me. Honor my prayers by honoring Your own words. I praise You and pray to You in the name of Jesus. Amen.

**God, in accordance
with Your word . . .**

I pray that while my spouse and I have not seen You, God, at any time, if we love one another, You abide in us, and Your love has been perfected in us.

1 JOHN 4:12

I pray, Jesus, that my spouse and I will follow Your commandment, that we love one another as You have loved us.

JOHN 15:12

I pray that if You, God, so loved my spouse
and me, we also ought to love one another.

1 JOHN 4:11

———— ∞ ————

I pray, Lord Jesus, that by this my spouse
and I know love, because You laid down
Your life for us. And we also ought to lay
down our lives for the brethren.

1 JOHN 3:16

———— ∞ ————

I pray, Lord God, that my spouse and I will
love one another, for love is of You; and
everyone who loves is born of You and
knows You. But if we do not love, we do
not know You, for You are love.

1 JOHN 4:7–8

———— ∞ ————

I pray, Jesus, that my spouse and I will follow
Your command that we love one another.

JOHN 15:17

I pray, Lord Jesus, that my spouse and I always remember that when we were still without strength, in due time You died for us.

ROMANS 5:6

———— ∞ ————

I pray that my spouse and I will always understand the significance of the question, "Can two walk together, unless they are agreed?"

AMOS 3:3

28
MARITAL PROBLEMS

God, I love my spouse. But sometimes things aren't right in our marriage. Neither of us wants that. Hear the words that follow. They are Your words, and I pray them over any problems that might exist now or in the future in our marriage. Thank You, God, in Jesus' name for hearing and answering these my prayers. Amen.

God, in accordance
with Your word . . .

I pray that as for my spouse's and my house, we will serve the LORD.

JOSHUA 24:15

———————— ∞ ————————

I pray that my spouse and I have read that You, the LORD God said, "It is not good that man should be alone; I will make him a helper comparable to him."

GENESIS 2:18

I pray that my spouse and I always
understand that a man shall leave his
father and mother and be joined to his wife,
and they shall become one flesh.

GENESIS 2:24

I pray, God, that my spouse and I will let
all bitterness, wrath, anger, clamor, and
evil speaking be put away from us, with all
malice. And that we will be kind to one
another, tenderhearted, forgiving one
another, just as God in Christ forgave us.

EPHESIANS 4:31

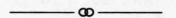

I pray that my spouse and I will behave
wisely in a perfect way. We will walk
within our house with a perfect heart.

PSALM 101:2

I pray that my spouse and I remember that
hatred stirs up strife, but love covers all
sins.

PROVERBS 10:12

I pray that my spouse and I will be of one
mind, having compassion for one another;
love as brothers, be tenderhearted, be
courteous; not returning evil for evil or
reviling for reviling, but on the contrary
blessing, knowing that we were called to
this, that we may inherit a blessing.

1 PETER 3:8–9

I pray that my spouse and I will trust in You,
the LORD, with all our hearts, and lean
not on our own understanding; and in all
our ways acknowledge You, and You shall
direct our paths.

PROVERBS 3:5–6

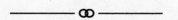

I pray that since my spouse and I have
purified our souls in obeying the truth
through the Spirit in sincere love of the
brethren, that we will love one another
fervently with a pure heart.

1 PETER 1:22

29

MARGIAGE

Lord Jesus, our marriage is important. It's important to You and it's important to us. Help us to have a wonderful marriage. And help us to always remember to pray Your words that follow for our marriage. And please grant us positive answers to these prayers. Amen.

God, in accordance
with Your word . . .

I pray that my spouse and I will not depart from each other.

1 CORINTHIANS 7:10

———— ∞ ————

I pray that my spouse and I will love each other and our children.

TITUS 2:4

I pray that as the elect of God, holy and beloved, that my spouse and I put on tender mercies, kindness, humility, meekness, longsuffering; bearing with one another, and forgiving one another, if we have a complaint against each other; even as Christ forgave us, so we also must do. But above all these things, help us to put on love, which is the bond of perfection.

COLOSSIANS 3:12–14

30

NEEDS

Lord God, You and only You know all of the needs that my spouse and I have. And only You can meet those needs. Now I want to pray Your word to You and to ask You to meet our needs through the power vested in Your perfect word. Thank You in Jesus' name for hearing and answering my prayers. Amen.

God, in accordance with Your word . . .

I pray that my spouse and I will delight ourselves also in You, the LORD, and You shall give us the desires of our hearts.

PSALM 37:4

———————— ∞ ————————

I pray that You, the LORD, will guide my spouse and me continually.

ISAIAH 58:11

I pray that You, God, will open Your hand and satisfy the desires of my spouse and myself.

PSALM 145:16

———— ∞ ————

I pray that my spouse and I will not spend wages for what does not satisfy and that we will listen carefully to You, God, and will let our souls delight themselves in abundance.

ISAIAH 55:2

———— ∞ ————

I pray that whatever things my spouse and I ask in prayer, believing, we will receive.

MATTHEW 21:22

———— ∞ ————

I pray, Jesus, that if my spouse and I ask anything in Your name, You will do it.

JOHN 14:14

I pray, Lord Jesus, that if my spouse and I abide in You, and Your words abide in us, we will ask what we desire, and it shall be done for us.

JOHN 15:7

—— ∞ ——

I pray that my spouse and I will ask in Your name, Jesus, and we will receive, that our joy may be full.

JOHN 16:24

—— ∞ ——

I pray that my spouse and I shall know the truth, and the truth shall make us free.

JOHN 8:32

—— ∞ ——

I pray that You, the God and Father of our Lord Jesus Christ, have blessed us with every spiritual blessing in the heavenly places in Christ.

EPHESIANS 1:3

I pray that my spouse and I can do all things through You, Christ, who strengthen us.

PHILIPPIANS 4:13

I pray that You, my God, shall supply all our needs according to Your riches in glory by Christ Jesus.

PHILIPPIANS 4:19

I pray that if my spouse's and my hearts do not condemn us, we have confidence toward You, God, and whatever we ask we receive from You, because we keep Your commandments and do those things that are pleasing in Your sight.

1 JOHN 3:21–22

31

OBEDIENCE

Lord, Your word says that our obedience is more important to You than sacrifice. I now pray to You and ask that You teach my spouse and me total obedience to You and Your word. I pray Your words to You in Jesus' name. Amen.

**God, in accordance
with Your word . . .**

I pray that my spouse and I recognize that You, God, have set before us today a blessing and a curse: the blessing, if we obey Your commandments which You command us today; and the curse, if we do not obey Your commandments, but turn aside from the way which You command us today, to go after other gods which we have not known.

DEUTERONOMY 11:26–28

I pray that my spouse and I never forget
that to obey is better than sacrifice.

1 SAMUEL 15:22

———— ∞ ————

I pray that my spouse and I will heed Your
commandments, O God, that our peace
will be like a river, and our righteousness
like the waves of the sea.

ISAIAH 48:18

———— ∞ ————

I pray, O God, that my spouse and I will
obey Your voice, and You will be our God,
and we shall be Your people. And that we
will walk in all the ways that You have
commanded us, that it may be well with us.

JEREMIAH 7:23

———— ∞ ————

I pray, Lord Jesus, that my spouse and I will
always love You and keep Your
commandments.

JOHN 14:15

I pray, God, that my spouse and I know that we ought to obey You rather than men.

ACTS 5:29

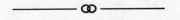

I pray, Jesus, that my spouse and I will always keep Your commandments.

1 JOHN 2:3

I pray that my spouse and I will walk in Your ways, to keep Your statutes and Your commandments, and that You will lengthen our days.

1 KINGS 3:14

I pray that You, God, will teach my spouse and me to do Your will, for You are our God.

PSALM 143:10

I pray that my spouse and I will learn Your
statutes, O God, and be careful to observe
them. I pray that we shall be careful to do
as You have commanded us and that we
shall not turn aside to the right hand or to
the left. I pray that we shall walk in all
the ways which You have commanded us,
that we may live and that it may be well
with us, and that we may prolong our days.

DEUTERONOMY 5:1, 32–33

I pray that whatever my spouse and I do,
we do it heartily, as to You and not to
men.

COLOSSIANS 3:23

32

PATICENCE

Jesus, patience is so important in the Christian life that my spouse and I desire to live. Honor these prayers of Your words and teach us patience. In Your name I pray. Amen.

God, in accordance
with Your word . . .

I pray that my spouse and I will imitate those who through faith and patience inherit the promises.

HEBREWS 6:12

I pray that my spouse and I do not cast away our confidence, which has great reward. For we have need of endurance, so that after we have done Your will, we may receive the promise.

HEBREWS 10:35–36

I pray that whatever things were written before were written for my spouse's and my learning, that we through the patience and comfort of the Scriptures might have hope. Now may You, the God of patience and comfort, grant us to be like-minded toward one another, according to Your Son, Christ Jesus.

ROMANS 15:4–5

———— ∞ ————

I pray that my spouse and I will rest in You, LORD, and wait patiently for You. I pray that we do not fret because of him who prospers in his way, because of the man who brings wicked schemes to pass. I pray that we will cease from anger, and forsake wrath, and that we do not fret—it only causes harm.

PSALM 37:7–8

———— ∞ ————

I pray that my spouse and I will wait patiently for You, LORD, and that You will incline Yourself to us, and hear our cry.

PSALM 40:1

I pray that my spouse and I will glory in tribulations, knowing that tribulation produces perseverance; and perseverance, character; and character, hope.

ROMANS 5:3–4

I pray that since my spouse and I are surrounded by so great a cloud of witnesses, let us lay aside every weight, and the sin which so easily ensnares us, and let us run with endurance the race that is set before us.

HEBREWS 12:1

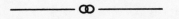

I pray that my spouse and I will wait on You, LORD, and that we shall renew our strength. I pray that my spouse and I shall mount up with wings like eagles, and we shall run and not be weary, we shall walk and not faint.

ISAIAH 40:31

I pray that my spouse and I will not hasten
in our spirits to be angry, for anger rests
in the bosom of fools.

ECCLESIASTES 7:9

———————— ∞ ————————

I pray that the fruit of the Spirit in my spouse
and me is love, joy, peace, longsuffering,
kindness, goodness, faithfulness, gentleness,
self-control.

GALATIANS 5:22–23

———————— ∞ ————————

I pray that my spouse and I wait on You,
Lord, and that we will be of good courage,
and You shall strengthen our hearts and that
we will wait on You.

PSALM 27:14

———————— ∞ ————————

I pray that my spouse and I will hope and
wait quietly for the salvation of the Lord.

LAMENTATIONS 3:26

I pray that my spouse and I will hope for what we do not see, and eagerly wait for it with perseverance.

ROMANS 8:25

———— ∞ ————

I pray that my spouse and I understand that the testing of our faith produces patience. And that we let patience have its perfect work, that we may be perfect and complete, lacking nothing.

JAMES 1:3–4

———— ∞ ————

I pray that my spouse and I will be patient until Your coming, Lord. I pray that my spouse and I will see how the farmer waits for the precious fruit of the earth, waiting patiently for it until it receives the early and latter rain and that we also will be patient, for Your coming is near.

JAMES 5:7–8

33

PEACE

Heavenly Father, peace is so important to my spouse and me. Only You can provide real and lasting peace. That is my prayer as I pray Your words back to You. Please hear and answer my prayers which are Your words and Your perfect will for us. In Jesus' name I pray. Amen.

God, in accordance
with Your word . . .

I pray that You will keep my spouse and me
in perfect peace, whose minds are stayed
on You, because we trust in You.

ISAIAH 26:3

———————— ∞ ————————

I pray that Your kindness, God, shall not
depart from us, nor Your covenant of
peace be removed from us.

ISAIAH 54:10

I pray that my spouse and I will both lie down in peace, and sleep; for You alone, O Lord, make us dwell in safety.

PSALM 4:8

I pray, O Lord, that You will give strength to my spouse and me and that You will bless us with peace.

PSALM 29:11

I pray that You, Jesus, have left Your peace with my spouse and me. I pray that our hearts will not be troubled, neither will we be afraid.

JOHN 14:27

I pray that my spouse and I, who have been justified by faith, will have peace with You, God, through Your Son, our Lord Jesus Christ.

ROMANS 5:1

I pray that You, Jesus, are my spouse's and
my peace.

EPHESIANS 2:14

I pray that my spouse and I will be anxious
for nothing, but in everything by prayer
and supplication, with thanksgiving, will let
our requests be made known to You; and
Your peace, which surpasses all
understanding, will guard our hearts and
minds through Your Son, Christ Jesus.

PHILIPPIANS 4:6–7

I pray, God, that the peace of God rules in
my spouse's and my hearts.

COLOSSIANS 3:15

34

POWER

Lord, my spouse and I need Your power in our marriage and in our individual lives. We have no power without You. My prayers are Your own words and I ask You now to honor them. Thank You, in Jesus' name. Amen.

God, in accordance with Your word . . .

I pray that my spouse and I will take pleasure in infirmities, in reproaches, in needs, in persecutions, in distresses, for Christ's sake. For when we are weak, then we are strong.

2 CORINTHIANS 12:10

I pray that my spouse and I can do all things through You, Christ, who strengthen us.

PHILIPPIANS 4:13

I pray that in all these things my spouse and
I are more than conquerors through You
who loved us.

ROMANS 8:37

———— ∞ ————

I pray that You, God, are able to make all
grace abound toward my spouse and me,
that we, always having all sufficiency in all
things, may have an abundance for every
good work.

2 CORINTHIANS 9:8

———— ∞ ————

I pray, Jesus, that Your grace is sufficient for
us, for Your strength is made perfect in
weakness.

2 CORINTHIANS 12:9

———— ∞ ————

I pray that my spouse and I will see the
exceeding greatness of power toward us
who believe, according to the working of
Your mighty power.

EPHESIANS 1:19

I pray, Jesus, that whatever we ask in Your name, that You will do, that Your Father may be glorified in the Son.

JOHN 14:13

I pray, O God, that You are able to do exceedingly abundantly above all that we ask or think, according to the power that works in us.

EPHESIANS 3:20

35

PRAISE

Lord God, my spouse and I need to praise You more. In the prayers that follow, we ask You to fill us with praise for You and for Jesus and for the Holy Spirit. Fill us with praise in the wonderful name of Jesus, our Lord and our Savior. Amen.

God, in accordance with Your word . . .

I pray that my spouse and I will sing praises to You, God, who dwells in Zion, and that we will declare Your deeds among the people.

PSALM 9:11

———— ∞ ————

I pray that my spouse and I will sing to You, LORD, as long as we live; we will sing praise to our God while we have our being.

PSALM 104:33

I pray that every day my spouse and I will bless You, and we will praise Your name forever and ever.

PSALM 145:2

—————— ∞ ——————

I pray that my spouse and I will know that great are You, and greatly to be praised; and Your greatness is unsearchable.

PSALM 145:3

—————— ∞ ——————

I pray that my spouse's and my tongues shall speak of Your righteousness and of Your praise all the day long.

PSALM 35:28

—————— ∞ ——————

I pray that You will open my spouse's and my lips, and that our mouths shall show forth Your praise.

PSALM 51:15

I pray that my spouse and I will praise You.

ISAIAH 12:1

∞

I pray that my spouse and I will give You
thanks, O Lord God Almighty, You who
are and who was and who are to come,
because You have taken Your great power
and reigned.

REVELATION 11:17

∞

I pray that my spouse and I will hope
continually, and will praise You yet more
and more.

PSALM 71:14

∞

I pray, God, that my spouse and I will enter
into Your gates with thanksgiving, and into
Your courts with praise.

PSALM 100:4

I pray that You, LORD, are my spouse's and my strength and song, and that You have become our salvation; You are our God, and we will praise You.

EXODUS 15:2

—————— ∞ ——————

I pray that my spouse and I will proclaim the name of the LORD and ascribe greatness to our God.

DEUTERONOMY 32:3

—————— ∞ ——————

I pray that my spouse and I will proclaim, "The LORD lives! Blessed be my Rock! Let God be exalted, the Rock of my salvation!"

2 SAMUEL 22:47

—————— ∞ ——————

I pray that my spouse and I always remember that You, the LORD, are great and greatly to be praised.

1 CHRONICLES 16:25

I pray that my spouse and I will bless You,
the LORD, at all times; and that Your praise
continually be in our mouths.

PSALM 34:1

I pray, God, that You have put a new song
in my spouse's and my mouths—praise
to our God.

PSALM 40:3

I pray that my spouse and I realize that great
is the LORD, and greatly to be praised.

PSALM 48:1

I pray that my spouse and I pray, "Blessed
be the LORD, who daily loads us with
benefits."

PSALM 68:19

I pray that my spouse and I will give thanks
to You, LORD, for You are good! For Your
mercy endures forever.

PSALM 106:1

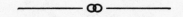

I pray that my spouse's and my souls live,
O God, and they shall praise You.

PSALM 119:175

I pray that my spouse and I will praise You,
God, for we are fearfully and wonderfully
made; marvelous are Your works, and that
our souls know very well.

PSALM 139:14

I pray that my spouse and I will praise You,
God, for Your mighty acts and that we
will praise You according to Your excellent
greatness!

PSALM 150:2

I pray that my spouse's and my mouths shall speak the praise of You, God.

PSALM 145:21

I pray that my spouse and I will praise You, the LORD!

PSALM 146:1

I pray that my spouse and I will continually offer the sacrifice of praise to You, God, that is, the fruit of our lips, giving thanks to Your name.

HEBREWS 13:15

36

PROTECTION

Jesus, I pray the very words and thoughts of God for the holy protection of my spouse and myself. Honor my prayers and surround us with Your angels. Please keep us from all evil and all evil from us. For it is in Your name that I pray. Amen.

God, in accordance with Your word . . .

I pray that our LORD God, who goes before my spouse and myself, will fight for us.

DEUTERONOMY 1:30

———————— ∞ ————————

I pray that if my spouse and I will indeed obey Your voice, God, and do all that You speak, then You will be an enemy to our enemies and an adversary to our adversaries.

EXODUS 23:22

I pray that no weapon formed against my spouse and me shall prosper, and that every tongue which rises against us in judgment You shall condemn.

ISAIAH 54:17

———— ∞ ————

I pray that Jesus has given my spouse and me authority to trample on serpents and scorpions, and over all the power of the enemy, and nothing shall by any means hurt us.

LUKE 10:19

———— ∞ ————

I pray that You, Lord, are faithful, who will establish my spouse and me and guard us from the evil one.

2 THESSALONIANS 3:3

———— ∞ ————

I pray that if God is for my spouse and me, who can be against us?

ROMANS 8:31

37

REBELLIOUS

Heavenly Father, by the praying of Your word I ask You to keep all rebellion from my spouse and me. Help us through Your word to recognize the first signs of rebellion in our lives and to rid ourselves of it through Your Son, for it is in Jesus' name that I pray. Amen.

God, in accordance with Your word . . .

I pray that my spouse and I, by doing good, may put to silence the ignorance of foolish men.

1 PETER 2:15

———— ∞ ————

I pray that if my spouse and I are willing and obedient, we shall eat the good of the land.

ISAIAH 1:19

I pray that my spouse and I will gird up the loins of our minds, be sober, and rest our hope fully upon the grace that is to be brought to us at the revelation of Jesus Christ; as obedient children, not conforming ourselves to the former lusts, as in our ignorance; but as You, God, who called us are Holy, we also are to be holy in all our conduct.

1 PETER 1:13–15

I pray that my spouse and I are aware that rebellion is as the sin of witchcraft.

1 SAMUEL 15:23

I pray that my spouse and I will obey those who rule over us, and be submissive, for they watch out for our souls, as those who must give account.

HEBREWS 13:17

I pray that my spouse and I will be like Jesus and humble ourselves and become obedient.

PHILIPPIANS 2:8

I pray that like You, Jesus, my spouse and I learn obedience by the things which we suffer.

HEBREWS 5:8

I pray, God, that my spouse and I know that You resist the proud, but give grace to the humble and that we will humble ourselves under Your mighty hand, that You may exalt us in due time.

1 PETER 5:5–6

I pray that my spouse and I know and understand that no grave trouble will overtake the righteous, but the wicked shall be filled with evil.

PROVERBS 12:21

I pray that my spouse and I will submit to
You, God. That we will resist the devil and
he will flee from us.

JAMES 4:7

I pray that while my spouse and I were once
darkness, but now we are light in the Lord
and that we will walk as children of light.

EPHESIANS 5:8

I pray that my spouse and I do not let sin
reign in our mortal bodies, that we should
obey it in its lusts. I also pray that we do
not present our members as instruments
of unrighteousness to sin, but present
ourselves to You, God, as being alive from
the dead, and our members as instruments
of righteousness to You. For sin shall not
have dominion over us, for we are not under
law but under grace.

ROMANS 6:12–14

I pray that my spouse and I will no longer walk as the rest of the Gentiles walk, in the futility of our minds.

EPHESIANS 4:17

38

SALVATION

Heavenly Father, in all of life there is nothing more important than our salvation. Bless now the praying of Your word for the salvation of my spouse and me. We have salvation through Your Son, and we pray in Jesus' name. Amen.

God, in accordance with Your word . . .

I pray that my spouse and I understand what You meant, Jesus, when You said, "He who believes in Me has everlasting life."

JOHN 6:47

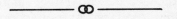

I pray that my spouse and I remember that You came to seek and to save that which was lost.

LUKE 19:10

I pray, Lord Jesus, that my spouse and I will come to understand what You meant when You said, "Therefore whoever confesses Me before men, him I will also confess before My Father who is in heaven."

MATTHEW 10:32

I pray that because my spouse and I confess with our mouths the Lord Jesus and believe in our hearts that You have raised Him from the dead, we will be saved. For with the heart one believes unto righteousness, and with the mouth confession is made unto salvation.

ROMANS 10:9–10

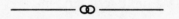

I pray that You, God, have saved my spouse and me and called us with a holy calling, not according to our works, but according to Your own purpose and grace which was given to us in Your Son, Christ Jesus, before time began.

2 TIMOTHY 1:9

I pray that You, God, so loved my spouse
and me that You gave Your only begotten
Son, that we who believe in Jesus should
not perish but have everlasting life.

JOHN 3:16

I pray, God, that You did not send Your Son
into the world to condemn the world, but
that the world through Jesus might be saved.

JOHN 3:17

I pray that this will be my spouse's and my
testimony: that You, God, have given us
eternal life, and this life is in Your Son.

1 JOHN 5:11

I pray that by grace my spouse and I have
been saved through faith, and that not
of ourselves; it is the gift of God, not of
works, lest anyone should boast.

EPHESIANS 2:8

I pray, God, that it is not by works of righteousness which my spouse and I have done, but according to Your mercy You saved us, through the washing of regeneration and renewing of the Holy Spirit, whom You poured out on us abundantly through Jesus Christ our Savior.

TITUS 3:5–6

———— ∞ ————

I pray, Jesus, that You stand at the door and knock and if my spouse and I hear Your voice and open the door, You will come in to us and dine with us, and us with You.

REVELATION 3:20

———— ∞ ————

I pray, God, that my spouse and I have been born again, not of corruptible seed but incorruptible, through Your word which lives and abides forever.

1 PETER 1:23

39

SATAN DEFEATED

Lord God, Satan is a terrible enemy to my spouse and me. But You who are in us are stronger and more powerful than Satan can ever be. At this time I come before You to pray Your words to overcome Satan's attacks on my spouse and me and our marriage. Honor Your word and drive our enemy far from us. In Jesus' name I pray. Amen and amen.

God, in accordance
with Your word . . .

I pray that my spouse and I will be strong in You, Lord, and in the power of Your might. I pray that we will put on Your whole armor, that we may be able to stand against the wiles of the devil. For we do not wrestle against flesh and blood, but against principalities, against powers, against the rulers of the darkness of this age, against spiritual hosts of wickedness in the heavenly places. I pray that we will take up Your

whole armor of God, that we may be able
to withstand in the evil day, and having
done all, to stand. I pray that my spouse and
I have girded our waists with truth, put
on the breastplate of righteousness, and shod
our feet with the preparation of the gospel
of peace; and above all, taking the shield
of faith with which we will be able to
quench all the fiery darts of the wicked one.
I pray that we also take the helmet of
salvation, and the sword of the Spirit, which
is Your word; praying always with all
prayer and supplication in the Spirit, being
watchful to this end with all perseverance
and supplication for all the saints.

EPHESIANS 6:10–18

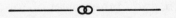

I pray that You, God, will open my spouse's
and my eyes, in order to turn us from
darkness to light, and from the power of
Satan to God, that we may receive
forgiveness of sins and an inheritance among
those who are sanctified by faith in Jesus.

ACTS 26:18

I pray that You preserve my spouse's and
my souls and deliver us out of the hand
of the wicked.

PSALM 97:10

I pray, God, for my spouse's and my lives
that the Son of God was manifested, that
He might destroy the works of the devil.

1 JOHN 3:8

I pray for my spouse and me that we put
off, concerning our former conduct, the
old man which grows corrupt according to
the deceitful lusts, and be renewed in the
spirit of our minds, and that we put on the
new man which was created according
to You, God, in true righteousness and
holiness.

EPHESIANS 4:22–24

I pray, Jesus, that my spouse and I know that
You have disarmed principalities and
powers, and have made a public spectacle
of them, triumphing over them in it.

COLOSSIANS 2:15

———— ∞ ————

I pray, God, that my spouse and I understand
that even the angels who did not keep
their proper domain, but left their own
abode, You have reserved in everlasting
chains under darkness for the judgment of
the great day.

JUDE 1:6

———— ∞ ————

I pray that my spouse and I are strong, and
the word of God abides in us, and we
have overcome the wicked one.

1 JOHN 2:14

———— ∞ ————

I pray that my spouse and I will not give
place to the devil.

EPHESIANS 4:27

I pray that my spouse and I will submit to
You, God, and that we will resist the devil
and he will flee from us.

JAMES 4:7

I pray that my spouse and I will be sober
and vigilant; because our adversary the
devil walks about like a roaring lion, seeking
whom he may devour. I pray that we will
resist him, steadfast in the faith, knowing
that the same sufferings are experienced
by our brotherhood in the world.

1 PETER 5:8–9

I pray that at this time my spouse and I will
remember that You, Jesus, went about
doing good and healing all who were
oppressed by the devil, for Your Father
was with You.

ACTS 10:38

I do not pray, God, that You should take my
spouse and me out of the world, but that
You should keep us from the evil one.

JOHN 17:15

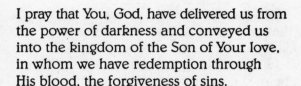

I pray that You, God, have delivered us from
the power of darkness and conveyed us
into the kingdom of the Son of Your love,
in whom we have redemption through
His blood, the forgiveness of sins.

COLOSSIANS 1:13–14

I pray that in all these things my spouse and
I are more than conquerors through You
who loved us.

ROMANS 8:37

I pray, God, that the accuser of my spouse
and me, who accuses us before You, God,
day and night, has been cast down. And I

pray that we overcame him by the blood
of the Lamb and by the word of our
testimony.

REVELATION 12:10–11

I pray that neither death nor life, nor angels
nor principalities nor powers, nor things
present nor things to come, nor height nor
depth, nor any other created thing, shall
be able to separate my spouse and me from
the love of God which is in Christ Jesus
our Lord.

ROMANS 8:38–39

I pray that while my spouse and I are hard
pressed on every side, yet not crushed;
we are perplexed, but not in despair;
persecuted, but not forsaken; struck down,
but not destroyed—always carrying about
in our bodies Your dying, Lord Jesus, that
Your life also may be manifested in our
bodies.

2 CORINTHIANS 4:8–10

I pray that though my spouse and I walk in the flesh, we do not war according to the flesh. For the weapons of our warfare are not carnal but mighty in God for pulling down strongholds, casting down arguments and every high thing that exalts itself against the knowledge of God, bringing every thought into captivity to the obedience of Christ.

2 CORINTHIANS 10:3–5

———— ∞ ————

I pray that my spouse and I have our senses exercised to discern both good and evil.

HEBREWS 5:14

———— ∞ ————

I pray, Lord, that You will guard my spouse and me from the evil one.

2 THESSALONIANS 3:3

———— ∞ ————

I pray, God, that Your presence will go with my spouse and me forever.

EXODUS 33:14

I pray, God, that my spouse and I will be
strong and of good courage; that we are
not afraid, nor dismayed, for You, the LORD
our God, are with us wherever we go.

JOSHUA 1:9

—————— ∞ ——————

I pray, God, that You will preserve the souls
of my spouse and me and that You will
deliver us out of the hand of the wicked.

PSALM 97:10

—————— ∞ ——————

I pray, God, that You are my spouse's and
my refuge and that You will thrust out
the enemy from before us.

DEUTERONOMY 33:27

—————— ∞ ——————

I pray, God, that the angel of the LORD
encamps all around my spouse and me
who fear You, and delivers us.

PSALM 34:7

I pray that Satan will not take advantage of my spouse and me; for we are not ignorant of his devices.

2 CORINTHIANS 2:11

I pray, Lord, that my spouse and I will drive Satan away by worshiping You, Lord, our God, and serving only You.

MATTHEW 4:10

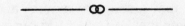

I pray that my spouse and I will gird up the loins of our mind, be sober, and rest our hope fully upon the grace that is to be brought to us at the revelation of Jesus Christ; as obedient children, not conforming ourselves to the former lusts, as in our ignorance; but as You, God, who called us are holy, may we also be holy in all our conduct.

1 PETER 1:13–15

I pray that my spouse and I know that we
do not live by bread alone but by every
word that proceeds from Your mouth, God.

MATTHEW 4:4

I pray that my spouse and I will have the
mind of Christ.

1 CORINTHIANS 2:16

40
SECURITY

~

Father in Heaven, the only real security that my
spouse and I can ever have comes from You. Jesus
is our security and I pray now Your words to ask for
that security now and forevermore. And I ask it in
Jesus' name. Amen.

God, in accordance
with Your word . . .

I pray that surely goodness and mercy shall
follow my spouse and me all the days of
our lives; and we will dwell in the house of
the LORD forever.

PSALM 23:6

———— ∞ ————

I pray that my spouse and I are two of those
who have come to You, Jesus, and whom
You will by no means cast out.

JOHN 6:37

I pray that neither death nor life, nor angels nor principalities nor powers, nor things present nor things to come, nor height nor depth, nor any other created thing, shall be able to separate my spouse and me from the love of God which is in Christ Jesus our Lord.

ROMANS 8:38–39

I pray that in Jesus my spouse and I also trusted, after we heard the word of truth, the gospel of our salvation; in whom also, having believed, we were sealed with the Holy Spirit of promise.

EPHESIANS 1:13

I pray, Jesus, that my spouse and I have heard Your voice, and we know You, and we follow You, and You will give us eternal life, and we shall never perish.

JOHN 10:27–28

I pray that my spouse and I do not grieve
the Holy Spirit of God, by whom we were
sealed for the day of redemption.

EPHESIANS 4:30

—————— ∞ ——————

I pray that You, God, who have begun a
good work in my spouse and me will
complete it until the day of Jesus Christ.

PHILIPPIANS 1:6

—————— ∞ ——————

I pray, Lord, that Your faithfulness will
establish my spouse and me and guard
us from the evil one.

2 THESSALONIANS 3:3

—————— ∞ ——————

I pray that You, God, are able to keep us
from stumbling, and to present us faultless
before the presence of Your glory with
exceeding joy.

JUDE 1:24

41

SERVING GOD

Heavenly Father, it is my spouse's and my desire to serve You and to please You. That is what I want to pray about to You today. Hear Your very words and honor them. Help us to learn to serve You and to have a heart to serve You. These things I ask in Jesus' name. Amen.

God, in accordance with Your word . . .

I pray that my spouse and I shall walk after You, the LORD our God, and fear You, and keep Your commandments and obey Your voice, and we shall serve You and hold fast to You.

DEUTERONOMY 13:4

I pray that my spouse and I will worship You, the Lord our God, and You only we shall serve.

MATTHEW 4:10

I pray, God, that my spouse and I know that we cannot serve two masters; for either we will hate the one and love the other, or else we will be loyal to the one and despise the other. We cannot serve You and mammon.

MATTHEW 6:24

I pray that my spouse and I will always love You, the LORD our God, to walk in all Your ways, to keep Your commandments, to hold fast to You, and to serve You with all our hearts and with all our souls.

JOSHUA 22:5

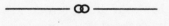

I pray to You, God, that my spouse and I will present our bodies a living sacrifice, holy, acceptable to God, which is our reasonable service. I pray also that we will not be conformed to this world, but be transformed by the renewing of our minds, that we may prove what is that good and acceptable and perfect will of God.

ROMANS 12:1–2

I pray that my spouse and I will be kindly
affectionate to others with brotherly love,
in honor giving preference to others; not
lagging in diligence, fervent in spirit,
serving You; distributing to the needs of the
saints, given to hospitality.

ROMANS 12:10–11, 13

I pray that my spouse and I do not turn aside
from following You, LORD, but serve You
with all our hearts. I pray that we do not
turn aside; for then we would go after
empty things which cannot profit or deliver,
for they are nothing. For You will not
forsake us, for Your great name's sake,
because it has pleased You, LORD, to make
us Your people.

1 SAMUEL 12:20–22

I pray, O God, that my spouse and I shall
serve You, the LORD our God.

EXODUS 23:25

I pray that my spouse and I will know You,
God, and serve You with loyal hearts and
with willing minds; for You search all hearts
and understand all the intent of the
thoughts. If we seek You, You will be found
by us; but if we forsake You, You will cast
us off forever.

1 CHRONICLES 28:9

I pray that my spouse and I have been
delivered from the law, having died to
what we were held by, so that we should
serve in the newness of the Spirit and not
in the oldness of the letter.

ROMANS 7:6

I pray that my spouse and I will serve You,
the LORD, with gladness and come before
Your presence with singing. I pray that we
will know that You, LORD, are God and
that it is You who have made us, and not
we ourselves.

PSALM 100:2–3

I pray that my spouse and I will fear You, the LORD our God, to walk in all Your ways and to love You, to serve You, the LORD our God, with all our hearts and with all our souls, and to keep Your commandments, LORD, and Your statutes which You command us today for our good.

DEUTERONOMY 10:12–13

42

SICKNESS

Lord Jesus, You are the Great Healer. Hear the words of Scripture as my prayers for the healing of any afflictions or illnesses that may now exist or may come into my spouse's or my life at any time in the future. In Your Holy name I thank You for hearing these my prayers. Amen.

God, in accordance with Your word . . .

I pray that You will heal my spouse and me, O LORD, and we shall be healed. Save us and we shall be saved.

JEREMIAH 17:14

I pray, God, that You will restore health to my spouse and me and heal our wounds.

JEREMIAH 30:17

I pray that my spouse and I will diligently heed Your voice, LORD God, and do what is right in Your sight, give ear to Your commandments and keep all Your statutes, and that You will put no diseases on us.

EXODUS 15:26

———— ∞ ————

I pray that we remember that You were wounded for my spouse's and my transgressions, You were bruised for our iniquities; and by Your stripes we are healed.

ISAIAH 53:5

———— ∞ ————

I pray that we remember, Jesus, that You Yourself bore my spouse's and my sins in Your own body on the tree, that we, having died to sins, might live for righteousness—by whose stripes we were healed.

1 PETER 2:24

I pray, God, that You heal my spouse's and my iniquities, heal all our diseases, and redeem our lives from destruction.

PSALM 103:3–4

———————— ⚭ ————————

I pray that my spouse and I may prosper in all things and be in health, just as our souls prosper.

3 JOHN 1:2

———————— ⚭ ————————

I pray, Jesus, that my spouse and I remember that You healed every sickness and every disease among the people.

MATTHEW 9:35

———————— ⚭ ————————

I pray, Jesus, that power goes out from You and heals my spouse and me.

LUKE 6:19

I pray, God, that my spouse and I remember
that You sent Your word and healed my
spouse and me, and delivered us from our
destructions.

PSALM 107:20

———— ∞ ————

I pray, God, that my spouse and I realize
we are not worthy that You should come
under our roof. But only speak a word, and
we will be healed.

MATTHEW 8:8

———— ∞ ————

I pray that the prayer of faith will save my
spouse and me from our sickness, and
the Lord will raise us up. And if we have
committed sins, we will be forgiven.

JAMES 5:15

43

SPIRITUAL GROWTH

Father God, the most powerful prayers that I can pray are Your words that reflect Your will for my spouse and me. Those very words are the words that I now pray as I petition You to help us to grow spiritually. Fill each of us with Your Spirit and help us to grow in Your ways. In Jesus' name I thank You. Amen.

God, in accordance with Your word . . .

I pray that my spouse and I will beware, lest there be in us an evil heart of unbelief in departing from the living God; I pray that we will exhort one another daily, while it is called "Today," lest we be hardened through the deceitfulness of sin.

HEBREWS 3:12–13

I pray, God, that my spouse and I will return to You, and You will return to us.

MALACHI 3:7

I pray that my spouse and I do not forget
You, the LORD our God, by not keeping Your
commandments, Your judgments, and Your
statutes which You command us today. I pray
that we shall remember You, the LORD our
God, for it is You who gives us the power
to get wealth.

DEUTERONOMY 8:11, 17

I pray that my spouse and I have not
forgotten Your name, or stretched out our
hands to a foreign god. Would You, God,
not search this out? For You know the secrets
of the heart.

PSALM 44:20–21

I pray, God, that my spouse and I will be
watchful, and strengthen the things which
remain, that are ready to die, for we have
not found our works perfect before You,
God.

REVELATION 3:2

I pray that my spouse and I will take heed
to ourselves, and diligently keep ourselves,
lest we forget the things our eyes have seen,
and lest they depart from our hearts all the
days of our lives.

DEUTERONOMY 4:9

I pray that my spouse and I will look
diligently lest we fall short of Your grace;
lest any root of bitterness springing up cause
trouble, and by this we become defiled.

HEBREWS 12:15

I pray that after my spouse and I have
escaped the pollutions of the world through
the knowledge of You, our Lord and Savior
Jesus Christ, we are not again entangled in
them and overcome.

2 PETER 2:20

44

STRENGTH

꘏

Lord God, grant through the praying of Your word
the strength that only You can give to my spouse
and me. Make us strong in the right places. Help us
to remember that Your strength is made perfect in
weakness. In Jesus' name I thank You for the strength
we have to overcome our weakness. Amen.

God, in accordance
with Your word . . .

I pray, God, that You give power to my
spouse and me who are weak, and to us
who have no might You increase strength.

ISAIAH 40:29

꘏

I pray that my spouse and I shall wait on
You, LORD, and we shall renew our strength;
we shall mount up with wings like eagles,
we shall run and not be weary, we shall walk
and not faint.

ISAIAH 40:31

I pray that my spouse and I will fear not, for You are with us; I pray that we will not be dismayed, for You are our God. I pray that You will strengthen us, yes, that You will help us, You will uphold us with Your righteous right hand.

ISAIAH 41:10

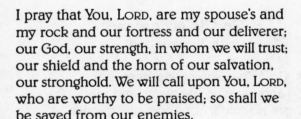

I pray that You, LORD, are my spouse's and my rock and our fortress and our deliverer; our God, our strength, in whom we will trust; our shield and the horn of our salvation, our stronghold. We will call upon You, LORD, who are worthy to be praised; so shall we be saved from our enemies.

PSALM 18:2–3

I pray that You, LORD, are my spouse's and my light and our salvation; whom shall we fear?

PSALM 27:1

I pray that my spouse and I can do all things
through You, Christ, who strengthen us.

PHILIPPIANS 4:13

I pray that You, God, will grant my spouse
and me, according to the riches of Your
glory, to be strengthened with might through
Your Spirit.

EPHESIANS 3:16

I pray that my spouse and I will be strong
in You, Lord, and in the power of Your might.
I pray that we will put on Your whole armor,
that we may be able to stand against the
wiles of the devil. For we do not wrestle
against flesh and blood, but against
principalities, against powers, against the
rulers of the darkness of this age, against
spiritual hosts of wickedness in the heavenly
places.

EPHESIANS 6:10–12

I pray, God, that You will strengthen my spouse and me according to Your word.

PSALM 119:28

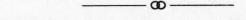

I pray, God, that my spouse and I will be strengthened with all might, according to Your glorious power.

COLOSSIANS 1:11

I pray that my spouse and I will take up Your whole armor, God, that we may be able to withstand in the evil day, and having done all, to stand. I pray that my spouse and I have girded our waists with truth, put on the breastplate of righteousness, and shod our feet with the preparation of the gospel of peace; and above all, taking the shield of faith with which we will be able to quench all the fiery darts of the wicked one. I pray that we also take the helmet of salvation, and the sword of the Spirit, which is Your

word; praying always with all prayer and
supplication in the Spirit, being watchful to
this end with all perseverance and
supplication for all the saints.

EPHESIANS 6:13–18

45

TEMPTED

Lord, I surround my spouse and myself with Your word. Use it to keep us from temptation. Use it to keep us pure. Honor Your word and my praying of Your word to deliver us from all temptation. In Jesus' name I pray. Amen.

God, in accordance with Your word . . .

I pray that You, Lord, know how to deliver my spouse and myself out of temptations.

2 PETER 2:9

─────── ∞ ───────

I pray that sin shall not have dominion over my spouse and me, for we are not under law but under grace.

ROMANS 6:14

I pray, LORD, that Your word my spouse and I have hidden in our hearts, that we might not sin against You.

PSALM 119:11

I pray, Lord, that my spouse and I will not say when we are tempted, "I am tempted by God"; for You cannot be tempted by evil, nor do You Yourself tempt anyone. But we are tempted when we are drawn away by our own desires and enticed.

JAMES 1:13–14

I pray that if my spouse and I confess and forsake our sins we will have mercy.

PROVERBS 28:13

I pray that if we confess our sins, You are faithful and just to forgive us our sins and to cleanse us from all unrighteousness.

1 JOHN 1:9

I pray that no temptation has overtaken my spouse and me except such as is common to man; but You, God, are faithful, and will not allow us to be tempted beyond what we are able, but with the temptation will also make the way of escape, that we may be able to bear it.

1 CORINTHIANS 10:13

I pray that my spouse and I know that we do not have a High Priest who cannot sympathize with our weaknesses, but was in all points tempted as we are, yet without sin. Let us therefore come boldly to the throne of grace, that we may obtain mercy and find grace to help in time of need.

HEBREWS 4:15–16

I pray, Jesus, that You are able to aid my spouse and me who are tempted.

HEBREWS 2:18

I pray that my spouse and I will be sober
and vigilant; because our adversary the devil
walks about like a roaring lion, seeking
whom he may devour. I pray that we will
resist him, steadfast in the faith, knowing
that the same sufferings are experienced by
our brotherhood in the world.

1 PETER 5:8–9

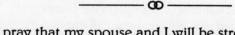

I pray that my spouse and I will be strong
in You, Lord, and in the power of Your might.
I pray that we will put on Your whole armor,
that we may be able to stand against the
wiles of the devil, and above all, taking the
shield of faith with which we will be able
to quench all the fiery darts of the wicked
one.

EPHESIANS 6:10–11, 16

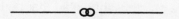

I pray, God, that my spouse and I will resist
the devil and he will flee from us.

JAMES 4:7

I pray that You who are in my spouse and me are greater than he who is in the world.

1 JOHN 4:4

I pray, Lord, that my spouse and I count it all joy when we fall into various trials, knowing that the testing of our faith produces patience. We who endure temptation are blessed; for when we have been approved, we will receive the crown of life which You have promised to those who love You.

JAMES 1:2–3, 12

I pray that in this my spouse and I greatly rejoice, though now for a little while, if need be, we have been grieved by various trials, that the genuineness of our faith, being much more precious than gold that perishes, though it is tested by fire, may be found to praise, honor, and glory at the revelation of Jesus Christ.

1 PETER 1:6–7

I pray that You, God, are able to keep my spouse and me from stumbling, and to present us faultless before the presence of Your glory with exceeding joy.

JUDE 1:24

46

TROUBLES

Lord God, I pray Your words over any troubles that my spouse and I face now or that we may face in the future. Your word is the sword of the Spirit in our lives and we pray it now to drive troubles far from us. Now, at this time, I pray Your words in Jesus' name. Amen.

**God, in accordance
with Your word . . .**

I pray that my spouse and I will be anxious for nothing, but in everything by prayer and supplication, with thanksgiving, let our requests be made known to You, God; and Your peace, which surpasses all understanding, will guard our hearts and minds through Your Son, Christ Jesus.

PHILIPPIANS 4:6–7

I pray that my spouse and I shall obtain joy and gladness; sorrow and sighing shall flee away.

ISAIAH 51:11

———————— ∞ ————————

I pray, God, that You will comfort my spouse and me in all our tribulation, that we may be able to comfort those who are in any trouble, with the comfort with which we ourselves are comforted by You.

2 CORINTHIANS 1:4

———————— ∞ ————————

I pray, God, that my spouse and I do not worry about tomorrow, for tomorrow will worry about its own things.

MATTHEW 6:34

———————— ∞ ————————

I pray that all things work together for good to my spouse and me who love You, God, to us who are the called according to Your purpose.

ROMANS 8:28

I pray that my spouse and I will be glad and rejoice in Your mercy, for You have considered our trouble; You have known our souls in adversities, and have not shut us up into the hand of the enemy; You have set our feet in a wide place.

PSALM 31:7–8

—————— ∞ ——————

I pray that my spouse's and my help comes from You, LORD, who made heaven and earth.

PSALM 121:2

—————— ∞ ——————

I pray that my spouse and I will come boldly to the throne of grace, that we may obtain mercy and find grace to help in time of need.

HEBREWS 4:16

—————— ∞ ——————

I pray, God, that my spouse and I will cast all our cares upon You, for You care for us.

1 PETER 5:7

I pray, O God, that my spouse and I will always remember that You are good, a stronghold in the day of trouble; and You know those who trust in You.

NAHUM 1:7

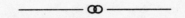

I pray that though my spouse and I are hard pressed on every side, yet we are not crushed; we are perplexed, but not in despair; persecuted, but not forsaken; struck down, but not destroyed.

2 CORINTHIANS 4:8–9

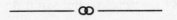

I pray, God, that when my spouse and I pass through the waters, You will be with us; and through the rivers, they shall not overflow us. When we walk through the fire, we shall not be burned, nor shall the flame scorch us. For You are the LORD our God.

ISAIAH 43:2–3

I pray that though my spouse and I walk in the midst of trouble, You will revive us; You will stretch out Your hand against the wrath of our enemies, and Your right hand will save us.

PSALM 138:7

I pray that my spouse and I will not let our hearts be troubled. I pray that we believe in You, God, and believe also in Your Son, Jesus.

JOHN 14:1

47

WAITING ON GOD

Heavenly Father, sometimes the most difficult thing for my spouse and me to do is to wait on You. Teach us, through the praying of Your word, to learn to wait on You. Help us to be patient until we hear from You. Thank You, in Jesus' name, for honoring these Your words. Amen.

God, in accordance
with Your word . . .

I pray, God, that my spouse and I will say in that day: "Behold, this is our God; we have waited for Him, and He will save us. This is the LORD; we have waited for Him; we will be glad and rejoice in His salvation."

ISAIAH 25:9

I pray that my spouse and I have become partakers of Christ if we hold the beginning of our confidence steadfast to the end.

HEBREWS 3:14

I pray that my spouse and I wait for You,
Lord, that our souls wait, and in Your word
we do hope.

PSALM 130:5

I pray that my spouse and I will wait on You,
Lord, and that we be of good courage, and
You shall strengthen our hearts.

PSALM 27:14

I pray, God, that my spouse's and my souls
wait silently for You alone, for our
expectation is from You.

PSALM 62:5

I pray that my spouse and I will hold fast
the confession of our hope without wavering,
for You who promised are faithful.

HEBREWS 10:23

I pray that my spouse and I shall wait on
You, LORD, and shall renew our strength;
we shall mount up with wings like eagles,
we shall run and not be weary, we shall walk
and not faint.

ISAIAH 40:31

I pray that my spouse's and my souls wait
for You, LORD, that You are our help and
our shield.

PSALM 33:20

48

WORRIED

Most Precious God, I pray Your very words over my spouse's and my worries. You have promised to not let our hearts be troubled if we will cast our cares on You. Based on Your words I pray that all worry will flee from us and that our joy will return to us. All of my prayers I pray in Jesus' name. Amen.

God, in accordance
with Your word . . .

I pray, God, that my spouse and I will not
let our hearts be troubled.

JOHN 14:1

——————— ∞ ———————

I pray that my spouse and I will both lie
down in peace, and sleep; for You alone,
O LORD, make us dwell in safety.

PSALM 4:8

I pray that my spouse and I will cast all our
cares upon You, for You care for us.

1 PETER 5:7

I pray that You, God, will keep my spouse
and me, whose minds are stayed on You,
in perfect peace, because we trust in You.

ISAIAH 26:3

I pray, God, that my spouse and I will let the
peace of God rule in our hearts.

COLOSSIANS 3:15

I pray that my spouse and I will be anxious
for nothing, but in everything by prayer and
supplication, with thanksgiving, let our
requests be made known to You, God; and
Your peace, which surpasses all
understanding, will guard our hearts and
minds through Christ Jesus.

PHILIPPIANS 4:6–7

I pray, God, that You shall supply all my
spouse's and my needs according to Your
riches in glory by Christ Jesus.

PHILIPPIANS 4:19

————— ∞ —————

I pray that my spouse and I will not worry
about our lives, what we will eat or what
we will drink; nor about our bodies, what
we will put on. I pray that we will seek first
Your kingdom, God, and Your righteousness,
and all these things shall be added to us.

MATTHEW 6:25, 33

————— ∞ —————

I pray, LORD, that when my spouse and I
lie down, we will not be afraid; yes, we will
lie down and our sleep will be sweet.

PROVERBS 3:24

————— ∞ —————

I pray that my spouse and I will say of You,
LORD, "He is my refuge and my fortress; my
God, in Him I will trust."

PSALM 91:2

I pray, O God, that great peace have my
spouse and I who love Your law, and nothing
causes us to stumble.

PSALM 119:165

———— ∞ ————

I pray, Jesus, that Your peace You leave with
my spouse and me, and that Your peace You
give to us; not as the world gives do You
give to us. Let not our hearts be troubled,
neither let them be afraid.

JOHN 14:27

Seminars conducted by Lee Roberts include *Praying God's Will, Avoiding Failure in Your Christian Walk,* and *The Businessman, the Salesman, and God!*

More information on these seminars can be obtained by writing Lee Roberts, P.O. Box 671465, Marietta, GA 30067-0025, or by calling 404-956-8550.